THE
POCKET
IDIOT'S
GUIDE™ TO

Play Groups

by Marian Edelman Borden

ALPHA

A member of Penguin Group (USA) Inc.

To my daughters-in-law, Rebecca Peters Borden and Jessica Weltman Borden, with much love and gratitude.

ALPHA BOOKS

Published by the Penguin Group

Penguin Group (USA) Inc., 375 Hudson Street, New York, New York 10014, USA

Penguin Group (Canada), 90 Eglinton Avenue East, Suite 700, Toronto, Ontario M4P 2Y3, Canada (a division of Pearson Penguin Canada Inc.)

Penguin Books Ltd., 80 Strand, London WC2R 0RL, England

Penguin Ireland, 25 St. Stephen's Green, Dublin 2, Ireland (a division of Penguin Books Ltd.)

Penguin Group (Australia), 250 Camberwell Road, Camberwell, Victoria 3124, Australia (a division of Pearson Australia Group Pty. Ltd.)

Penguin Books India Pvt. Ltd., 11 Community Centre, Panchsheel Park, New Delhi—110 017, India

Penguin Group (NZ), 67 Apollo Drive, Rosedale, North Shore, Auckland 1311, New Zealand (a division of Pearson New Zealand Ltd.)

Penguin Books (South Africa) (Pty.) Ltd., 24 Sturdee Avenue, Rosebank, Johannesburg 2196, South Africa

Penguin Books Ltd., Registered Offices: 80 Strand, London WC2R 0RL, England

Copyright © 2008 by Penguin Group (USA) Inc.

International Standard Book Number: 978-1-59257-805-4
Library of Congress Catalog Card Number: 2008922787

10 09 08   8 7 6 5 4 3 2 1

Interpretation of the printing code: The rightmost number of the first series of numbers is the year of the book's printing; the rightmost number of the second series of numbers is the number of the book's printing. For example, a printing code of 08-1 shows that the first printing occurred in 2008.

Printed in the United States of America

Note: This publication contains the opinions and ideas of its author. It is intended to provide helpful and informative material on the subject matter covered. It is sold with the understanding that the author and publisher are not engaged in rendering professional services in the book. If the reader requires personal assistance or advice, a competent professional should be consulted.

The author and publisher specifically disclaim any responsibility for any liability, loss, or risk, personal or otherwise, which is incurred as a consequence, directly or indirectly, of the use and application of any of the contents of this book.

Most Alpha books are available at special quantity discounts for bulk purchases for sales promotions, premiums, fund-raising, or educational use. Special books, or book excerpts, can also be created to fit specific needs.

For details, write: Special Markets, Alpha Books, 375 Hudson Street, New York, NY 10014.

Contents

Introduction

Both grown-ups and kids find their lives are richer, easier, and more fun when shared with friends. Play groups are a wonderful way for parents and children to connect. Formally organized or informal get-togethers, play groups offer moms and dads the opportunity to share good times and bad and fears and worries with others who are traveling the same parenting road. For children, a play group is the place to share giggles and toys, learn new skills, practice old ones, and just have fun.

Here, you'll find all the information you need to organize and enjoy a play group that works for both parents and kids. There is health information that parents should know before joining a play group. There are suggested activities for indoor and outdoor play, ideas for holiday and birthday celebrations, safety tips so that you can easily and quickly childproof the space in which you meet, and much more. There are also chapters containing information to help you resolve problems with children and with their parents. Find out why "play is the work of the child" and how much learning is really going on when kids are at play group.

While you are in the midst of toilet training and temper tantrums, wobbly first steps and sweet smiles, sticky fingers and hugs that cure boo-boos, take the wondrous journey with some friends who are also parents. Play groups put the focus on play for both grown-ups and kids.

Extras

In addition to the main text, this book includes three kinds of sidebars—each with a distinctive visual cue:

Play Group Do's

These tips give you fresh ideas or special information on child development and parenting.

Play Group Don'ts

These cautions alert you to safety concerns and help you avoid problems in your play group.

Play Group Chatter

These additional bits of information and advice from play group parents and other experts help make the experience more fun.

Acknowledgments

Thanks to the wonderful group at Alpha. I am especially indebted to Randy Ladenheim-Gil, who bought my very first book, and who has continued to offer wise counsel and encouragement through the years; to Lynn Northrup, the development editor for this project, who made the book much stronger with her careful line edits and perceptive suggestions; and to Janette Lynn, the production editor, whose attention to detail and the book's objectives kept this project on schedule and in focus.

Thanks, too, to Bob Diforio, agent extraordinaire.

I'm grateful to the many parents who shared their experiences and insights into the value, fun, and sometimes problems of play groups. I am thankful to the parents and kids of the play groups of my own four children. Their wisdom and support helped me navigate the tricky shoals of parenting, as well as enjoy the sheer delight of the experience. Finally, to my own family, this is written with much love for you all.

Trademarks

All terms mentioned in this book that are known to be or are suspected of being trademarks or service marks have been appropriately capitalized. Alpha Books and Penguin Group (USA) Inc. cannot attest to the accuracy of this information. Use of a term in this book should not be regarded as affecting the validity of any trademark or service mark.

The ABCs of Play Groups

In This Chapter

- What makes a play group?
- Having fun with other kids
- How play groups teach social skills
- Parents can benefit, too

There are lots of good reasons to join or create a play group for your child—not the least of which is that it will be fun for both you and your youngster! Whether your child is a baby, toddler, or preschooler, she'll enjoy being around other kids. The bonus is that you'll also benefit from interacting with other parents.

You and your child will both enjoy being part of a play group, even starting when your little one is just a few months old. Babies thrive and learn from the experience of being with other infants. According to Carollee Howes, professor of psychological studies in education at the University of California, Los Angeles, research has shown that "even at 10 to 12 months, toddlers can engage in common activities, such as peekaboo and crawl and chase."

These first friendships provide more than just companionship. They are learning experiences. "Social skills at this age, such as initiating contact and interacting with a peer, are pretty fragile. These little peekaboo games, even though they may seem simple to us, require a fair amount of sophistication on the part of the child," says Howes.

In this chapter, you'll learn the benefits for your child to being a member of a play group as well as what parents can get from these groups.

What Is a Play Group?

On a very basic level, play groups are just that: a bunch of kids getting together to play. But there's a lot going on behind that simple premise.

Play groups can run the gamut from formal to informal arrangements. In some groups, the parents stay during the play period; in others, a few adults are on duty while the rest have a few hours off while the kids play together. In still others, the parents hire a professional to coordinate the program but still require a parental time commitment when the group meets. Some programs are organized through an outside organization such as a church or newcomers club; others are loose affiliations with several parents agreeing to meet every Wednesday at the park, for example. Some groups meet in public spaces; most meet privately in members' homes.

ABC Play Group Chatter

For this book, I'm distinguishing between *play dates*, where your child plays one-on-one with another child, and *play groups*, which have a larger group of children and meet regularly.

The Fun Component

The bottom line is that kids like to play with other kids. Here's why. Early childhood friendships provide an outlet for all the energy that exhausts parents. As Professor Howes explains, "What mother wants to jump off a step 20 times?" On the other hand, two toddlers find that an irresistible game.

Joining a play group provides your child with built-in playmates. For the very little ones, it's parallel play—that is, the children play side by side but without any apparent interaction. Appearances can be deceiving, however. Even if your child seems oblivious to the baby next to him, it doesn't mean that he doesn't know that there is another child in the room. Deborah Lowe Vandell, professor of educational psychology at the University of Wisconsin, Madison, says, "Even infants as young as three or four months will look with interest at another baby. By six months, we can see babies playing rudimentary games with each other, such as looking at each other, smiling, laughing, and flapping their arms. I've also seen six-month-olds play squealing games with each other, where one baby squeals and the other infant squeals back, taking turns six or seven times."

Hopefully after a morning full of play, your child will be so exhausted that naptime—or at least a quiet period in the afternoon—is welcomed by both of you!

Play Group Do's

Take the initiative. Chat with other parents at the park. You can kick-start a more formally organized play group by first agreeing to meet other families at the playground at a scheduled time. This will give you a chance to check out the compatibility of the kids and parents.

Play Groups Promote Social Skills

Toddlers primarily engage in parallel play. Usually, it appears that they're more interested in the toy rather than the child clutching it. But these early play dates help build social skills. As Dr. Vandell explains, "Social interactions grow out of parallel play. You can't push it. They will interact at their own pace." By the time a child is four, he becomes more interested in interacting directly with his peers. Parallel play provides children an opportunity to learn through imitation.

Furthermore, the more time kids spend together, the more comfortable they become with each other and with new environments. Most children younger than three play better with someone they know than with a stranger.

Children in play groups also learn from the experience that their way of seeing the world isn't the only way. Being with other children and their families is an introduction to the concept that the world is bigger than their own homes. It teaches them that there is more than one way to play with a toy and solve a problem.

ABC Play Group Chatter

Douglas Nangle, associate professor of psychology at the University of Maine, studied the long-term effects of friendship and found that "Children's friendships are the training grounds for important adult relationships, including marriage."

Being in a play group also teaches children conflict resolution. At first, especially for little ones, parents need to model the appropriate behavior they want to teach. For example, you might say: "You want to play with the truck, and so does Jason. How about you take turns?" Or, "How about you get another truck and build a road for them together?" The goal is to help your child learn effective, appropriate techniques for resolving disputes.

Play groups also reinforce a child's language skills. The younger children mimic the language they hear around them. Older preschoolers learn quickly that they need to use words to communicate their preferences to peers.

Playing regularly with other kids also helps your child become more socially adept, according to a study by researchers at the University of Maine. It may also help your child's transition to kindergarten if he or she enters with at least one friend.

Peer pressure (the good kind) can also prompt the reluctant toddler to try using the potty or the fearful youngster to climb up the ladder to the slide. Friends build self-confidence—in children and in adults.

Grown-Up Benefits of Play Groups

Children are wonderful, delightful, and exhausting. But grown-ups need friends as much as little kids do. Parents often feel isolated and unsupported. Organizing a play group provides social opportunities for both parent and child. One study showed that one third of new mothers and fathers experience significant depression upon becoming parents. Joining a play group may make you feel less isolated and alone. Joining a play group when your child is just a baby may be even more valuable for you than for her. Other parents are the perfect resources for finding pediatricians, babysitters, and child-centric programs as well as advice on the best baby equipment, local parks, family-friendly restaurants, and more.

Play Group Don'ts

Sitter stealing is a play group no-no. If someone in your play group recommends her favorite sitter to you, don't monopolize the sitter's time or offer better rates. You may gain a caregiver but lose a friend.

Play groups also provide parents with the chance to share concerns and questions about child rearing with other people who are going through the same experiences. If you're convinced that your son will be 25 and still not toilet trained, you'll find a sympathetic ear at play group and some great tips on what works and what doesn't when potty training a child. Listening to how other parents have handled kids' problems will give you some much-needed perspective.

After you've spent days immersed in *Sesame Street* and *SpongeBob SquarePants*, it's refreshing to find other adults to chat with about things other than kid-related topics. The time in play group while the children are interacting gives parents a chance to connect with their peers as well. Knowing you will be with other adults may be the incentive you need to find the time to read a book and watch the news—or even just comb your hair and put on makeup. While it's reassuring to be able to chat about parental concerns with friends who are interested in the same topics, it's also revitalizing to be able to discuss grown-up subjects, too.

$A\!B\!C$ **Play Group Chatter**

My kids' play groups were a lifesaver for me. I wasn't working. I was at home with children, and those play groups provided me such comfort and friendship. The best and most lasting play group was surprisingly the one I had for my youngest. All of us had multiple kids. The kids played inside or outside. We bought donuts, made coffee, and talked and shared the most intimate details of our lives.

—Barbara, mother of three

Research has shown that friends help us get rid of stress. According to a study from researchers at the University of Florida, parents have significantly higher levels of depression than adults who don't have children. The assistance we get from family, friends, and our community can make the difference in dealing with pressures and problems. Having a friend you can turn to and who offers support is critical to both physical and mental health.

If your play group has both first-time and more experienced parents, you have the chance to learn from those who have recently been down the parenting road. They bring the much-needed "been there, done that" perspective. But unlike listening to grandparents, however well-meaning, these more experienced peers are in your generation.

They understand current medical and psychological issues. For example, parents with new babies understand the importance of putting a baby to sleep on his back (it reduces the risk of Sudden Infant Death Syndrome, [SIDS]). That's a different sleep protocol than your parents used for you.

Much like your child learns from playing with friends that his view of the world isn't the only one, through your play group you will have the opportunity to learn about different parenting styles. You may decide that your approach works best for both you and your family. But being in a play group lets you see other ways of dealing with issues—some of which might be worth a try.

Depending on how your play group is formed, it's also an opportunity to meet adults who you otherwise might never know. You are together based on common circumstances, not necessarily common interests. This gives you a chance to reach beyond your comfort zone and broaden your social group. Parenthood is the great equalizer.

Play Group Don'ts

When offering advice, whether it's on a parenting issue or a completely unrelated topic, don't take it personally if the other person chooses to ignore or reject your well-intended insight. Respect for differing points of view is the key to a successful play group.

Finally, having a play group is a great excuse to get out of the house—even if it's just once a week. Conversely, if it's your turn to host the play group, it's the perfect reason to clean up.

Play group parents forge strong bonds that often survive even if the kids outgrow each other. You've been in the preschool trenches with each other ... and not only survived, but thrived!

The Least You Need to Know

- A play group is usually organized by parents to provide their young children and themselves with opportunities for socializing.
- Infants and toddlers learn social skills as they parallel play alongside each other.
- Playing with their peers teaches preschoolers conflict resolution.
- Parents need opportunities to interact with other adults.

Let's Get Started

In This Chapter

- Starting your own play group
- How large should your group be?
- Play group supervision
- When, where, and how often to meet
- Tips for joining an existing play group
- Not for moms only!

Play groups provide kids and parents with fun, educational, and social opportunities. If a group is well organized, it can continue for years. Like any social group, however, there's the potential for hurt feelings and misunderstandings. You want to establish some clear ground rules so that everyone understands the expectations and responsibilities of group members.

In this chapter, we provide quick, easy steps for organizing a play group and making sure it runs smoothly as well as tips for deciding whether an existing play group is right for you.

Finding, Recruiting, and Keeping Members

To start your own play group, you first need to find members. Together, you can collectively decide the rules of the group: where, when, and how often you will meet. Take time to plan carefully so that everyone shares similar expectations.

You should hold an organizational meeting (discussed later in this chapter) to set up the structure of your play group. The ideas in this book are suggestions. They've worked for lots of groups, but be sure to tailor them to meet the needs of your members.

Who Makes a Good Play Group Member?

Finding the right mix of children and adults for the play group is essential. The children should be around the same age if possible. Even a few months makes a significant developmental difference, especially when they are very little.

Of course, it's unlikely that all the kids were born within the same week. For toddlers younger than two, try to keep the range within six months of the oldest to youngest. You can do a mixed-age grouping, but it requires close supervision and may limit some of the activities you can do with the group unless you have extra adults on hand to help the younger kids.

The age of the parents may or may not matter to you, but it's something to keep in mind. One of the reasons you want to form a play group is to find friends for your child but also for yourself. So, you may want to look for parents around the same age. Some older parents may prefer to see whether they can find a group where the parents are around their age. Similarly, a 20-something mother may feel less comfortable in a group where all the other parents are older than 40. Or, you may consider the age of the parents the least important issue. There may be other lifestyle questions that are of greater significance to you.

Gender-Balanced Play Groups?

Ideally, you would have the same number of boys and girls in the play group, but it's really not that important. Segregated play by gender becomes much more obvious as the children enter elementary school and becomes more pronounced by third grade.

In the meantime, even if the group is skewed with all boys and only one girl (or vice-versa), the type of play that's encouraged for preschoolers should be gender neutral. Both sexes enjoy nurturing stuffed animals, playing with blocks, cooking, painting, and playing dress-up and make-believe. Look for members whose company you enjoy.

Play Group Don'ts

Gender bias is often unintentional, but the effect is still detrimental. According to a report from the University of Wisconsin, Stevens Point, "Although most teachers believe that they treat girls and boys the same, research indicates that frequently they do not. Regardless of a teacher's gender, boys receive more teacher attention in the form of acceptance, praise, criticism, and remediation. Boys are given more time to talk in class from preschool through college."

Recruiting Members for the Play Group

Word of mouth is the easiest and least-expensive way to find families to join your play group. Start with people you know. Your child may already be playing with other kids, but now you're asking whether they want to formalize the arrangement.

You're not looking for carbon copies of yourself and your child. Diversity will enrich both your lives. On the other hand, be realistic. If the differences in child rearing or lifestyle will be a constant source of tension, then you probably want to find someone else for the group. Of course, if it's a stranger, you won't necessarily know ahead of time whether that person will be a good match for your group or not.

Here are some other suggestions for finding play group members:

- Advertise in the local community newspaper.
- Post a flyer on bulletin boards, such as in community centers, local supermarkets, libraries, and so on.
- Check the local hospital to see whether they have parenting classes and post a notice there.
- Insert a notice in your church/synagogue bulletin or homeowner's association newsletter.
- Ask the parents you met when you took your childbirth education class and/or prenatal exercise class.

The flyer should include the ages of the children wanted for the play group and the day and time of the organizational meeting. You can hold the meeting in your home, or you might choose to hold this organizational meeting in a public space, such as a coffee shop, church social hall, or library room. Include on the flyer either a telephone number or e-mail address so that interested families can RSVP.

If you opt for a daytime meeting, be prepared to have the kids there, too. You want to have toys available as well as snacks and refreshments for adults and children.

Play Group Do's

Some parents organize specialized play groups based on criteria other than the age of the child. Some groups are based on ethnicity, religion, single parents, first-time moms older than 40, adoptive moms, and more. Make your advertising clear about the type of group you're seeking.

The Organizational Meeting

There's a lot to discuss at this meeting. If you've taken the initiative to organize it, come prepared to lead the group through the series of decisions that need to be made. Before the meeting is over, the group should have made the following decisions:

- Size of the group
- Frequency of play group sessions
- Day(s) and time the group will meet
- Length of the sessions
- Where the group will meet
- Whether parents/caregivers will stay at each session (and if not, how many must be on duty)
- Basic structure of each session (free play, story time, snack time, art project?)

Everyone needs to be honest. It doesn't mean someone should be excluded, but you can only plan realistically if you have all the facts. For example, a parent whose child has a physical or mental handicap must be up-front about the youngster's needs. Or, a family who intends to send a babysitter to fulfill the parental obligations to the group must share that information with the members. The play group experience should be a success for every child as well as a fun experience for the adults.

In Chapter 4, I review health and safety issues the group must also address.

Play Group Do's

Create an online message board or e-mail list for your play group so members can check on any schedule changes or group alerts. Yahoo! Groups and MSN. com offer free message boards for groups. You may also want to create a phone chain, in case someone is not online to check e-mail.

Group Size: What's the Best Fit?

Deciding how large you want your play group to be is a tricky task. Play group size is more than a one-on-one play date but less than an unlimited open house.

On one hand, it's nice to be inclusive. If you're lucky enough to find a large number of parents eager to find a play group for their children, you don't want to leave anyone out. Plus, with the inevitable attrition on any given day as a result of illness, it's nice to have a large enough group that can still meet even if several children are ill.

On the other hand, especially for very young kids, too many people in a room can be overwhelming. Furthermore, there's the practical issue of finding spaces that can comfortably accommodate all the parents and children. Most importantly, there's the safety issue. Will you always have enough adults around to supervise—and, in the event of an emergency, get the children to safety?

Especially for children younger than two, limit the group size to between four and six children. But consider literally how many people will attend any given session if everyone shows up. For example, if you've organized the play group so at least two adults are always on duty—and you've decided to include siblings—then how many people will be in the room during the play group session? How many children will be competing for the same toy? Can you house that number of people comfortably? You can increase the number of children in the group as they get older.

Adult Supervision During Play Group

You can organize the group and create any schedule that works for all members. The only clear requirement is that the children are adequately supervised at all times.

Some groups decide that all parents/caregivers will stay at all group sessions. They enjoy the company.

But it's still wise to assign at least two parents to be on duty for each session. Those adults are in charge of preparing the snacks, organizing the morning's activity, and overseeing free play time.

Others choose to set up a rotating schedule, with some parents on duty and others free for a few hours. Again, depending on the age of the children, you need to be sure that you always have adequate supervision. You should have at least two adults on duty at all times. Here's a good rule of thumb: from birth to age 28 months, there should be at least 1 adult for every 3 children. As they get older, you can stretch the supervision to one adult for every four children. Always err on the side of caution. It's better to have too many adults on hand than too few. Be sure to factor in siblings in attendance when determining the adult-child ratio (discussed a little later in the chapter).

Parents Only?

You should also address whether you want a parents-only group. If part of the purpose of the play group is to make friends with other parents, you may want to limit the group to parents who will participate and not send a caregiver. This doesn't mean that you'd exclude working parents. One solution is to schedule the sessions on weekends so that parents can attend.

If you decide to structure the group so that there are two parents on duty each session and all others have a few hours off, then it's also possible that a parent may have some flexibility at work so that he or she can take a turn hosting the group (and in the other weeks, the caregiver drops off the child).

Your group may also decide that it doesn't matter who handles the family's play group responsibilities. Don't feel awkward raising this question, because it's important that everyone is honest about her concerns and preferences.

What About Siblings?

When you're calculating how many adults need to be on duty during a play group session, you need to consider how many children total will be in attendance. This means you must count not only the kids who are technically members of the group but also older and younger siblings who may come. The parent on duty can't rely on a younger sibling taking a nap during the session. Maintain the suggested adult-child ratio—even if the sibling is a newborn and won't be arguing over toys.

If you've decided to organize a mixed-age play group, make sure older siblings don't dominate play or toys. Similarly, if younger siblings attend, be careful that the available items are safe for younger kids. For example, smaller Lego pieces may be appropriate for four-year-olds but unsafe for a toddler.

Where to Meet

Where you choose to meet is a function of convenience and space. You want to make it easy for the members to get to and if necessary, park their cars near the playgroup. You also need to have a certain amount of space to house the children and adults.

At Members' Homes

The group may choose to meet in members' homes on a rotating basis. An important advantage of this system is that it permits each child to be the host—an important social lesson. We discuss in the next chapter how to help your child prepare for the occasions when it's his turn to share his toys and home.

No one needs to have a separate playroom or spacious digs in order to hold a play group. Kids don't care about the space, and nor should you (except that it's clean and safe). But you do need to be realistic. Ask members to consider the following for their homes:

- Is whatever room you choose to use large enough to accommodate all the kids, supervising adults, and toys?
- If additional adults will be present, can they sit in another room?
- Can you childproof the room you want to use? Can you safely blockade the area where you don't want children to go (for example, a workbench with tools)? Are household cleaning products out of reach?
- Is the space warm in the winter and cool in the summer? For example, if you decide to use an area of an unfinished basement, is it heated or warm enough?

Play Group Do's

When hosting a play group, add an area rug over a concrete basement floor for warmth and to cushion any falls.

Even if space is tight in your home, you may still be able to host a play group. Can you move the furniture against the walls to open a play space for the children? For example, can you move the coffee table out of the living room to open the center of the room? Can you push the dining table against the wall and move the chairs to another room? Or perhaps the children can play in your child's bedroom?

It's unwise—even if a member volunteers—to always hold the play group in the same person's home. It can become a burden to the parent, but even more it limits the opportunity for each child to welcome the others into her home. Moving the group from home to home also has the practical advantage of presenting a wider array of toys and experiences for the children.

Play Group Do's

It's very important, that each child has the opportunity to act as the host. That means if you structure your group so the host family provides snacks, then make sure every child shares that responsibility. The same would be true if the host child normally chooses the book to be read to the group. You want each child to have those special opportunities.

Using Public Spaces for a Play Group

If your group decides not to meet in private homes, there are public spaces you might consider. Check your library and community center to see whether they will permit you to use one of their rooms. Local churches and synagogues might also be willing to permit you to use some of their space.

Be sure to discuss the following issues:

- Any charges for the use of the room (and then discuss with the group how you will divide up the expenses)
- Whether you will be charged for weeks when the group doesn't meet (for example, during the holiday season)
- Whether the organization's insurance covers the use of the facilities by outside groups
- Whether childproofing materials are in place
- Availability of restroom facilities

- Security for your toys and supplies if you store them on-site
- Availability of kitchen facilities and use of their supplies (for example, pots, pans, pitchers, paper towels)
- Availability and fee for childcare workers and set-up if the format of the play group is that the children play in one room under supervision, while the parents meet in a separate room

If you can't store any materials at the site, divide up the responsibilities of bringing toys, snacks, and supplies to each group meeting. Make it clear that all members must either bring their assigned materials or arrange for them to be brought should they not plan to attend a play group session.

You may also choose to meet at a public playground. The disadvantages of this type of site are as follows:

- Inclement weather affects whether the play group meets and may discourage members from attending—even if the weather is iffy at first but then clears up.
- The group needs more supervising adults if the children are outside, especially in an unfenced area.
- You may not be able to do certain activities (like dress-up or puzzles) if you're at a playground.

- Children outside the playgroup may want to join the activities. You don't want to be responsible for other children or upset the social interaction of your play group.

Meeting Times

The group should agree on a consistent day and time to meet as well as session length. Children like predictability, and adults can include play group as part of their schedule. Changing days can be confusing and result in lower attendance.

How Often to Meet

Sessions meeting once a week or once every other week generally work best for most play groups. If the interval between meetings is much longer, younger children may not remember the group members and the adjustment period is extended. More frequent meetings are certainly possible but may be too demanding for most members' schedules. If possible, you want all group members to be able to attend—and most can arrange to be there once a week.

What Time of Day?

Especially for younger children, mornings are generally best. For those children younger than one year, scheduling a session for 10 A.M. allows the babies to have already taken their morning naps. They'll be rested and refreshed. It also gives parents/caregivers time to get ready and drive to the play group, as well as get older siblings off to school.

For toddlers and preschoolers who have given up napping twice a day, you might consider meeting at 10 A.M. or even slightly earlier.

Adults should discuss their children's nap schedules. Basically, you're looking to minimize crankiness—so you want a time period when the children are rested.

Play Group Do's

Your group may deliberately choose to meet during the weekend. This is especially helpful for parents whose work schedules don't permit them to attend a weekday play group.

How Long Is a Play Group Session?

The length of the play group sessions should be tied to the ages of the children. The stimulation of being with other kids, often in a strange environment (outside their own home), is exhausting.

For the youngest kids (younger than age two), keep the session to about 90 minutes or less. If you see that the children are growing fussy, shorten the sessions to an hour. Of course, you may lose 10 minutes on either end in the winter due to taking off and putting on coats, mittens, boots, hats, and so forth.

For older preschoolers, you can extend the sessions to two or two-and-a-half hours. Again, see how the kids are holding up. Parents need to judge whether it's productive to run the full length of a session.

Joining an Existing Play Group

It can be hard to join an existing play group—especially one that has been running for a long period of time. Like any other social situation, it's a little awkward because you're coming into the group when the other members, adults, and kids have already become friends and adjusted to each other. But with a little effort (on your part and the group's), you can make the transition easy and rewarding for both you and your child.

The advantage of joining a preexisting group is that the structure is already in place—and hopefully running smoothly. Of course, the disadvantage is that you won't have the opportunity to shape the structure of the play group—at least, not until you've been a member for a period of time and can begin to comfortably make suggestions.

One way you can judge whether the play group is right for you is to see how warm and welcoming members are when you first attend. Unless you are totally turned off by the experience, try attending a few sessions before making a final decision. First impressions can be misleading.

You can find existing play groups through word of mouth, from advertisements or notices in community newsletters, from notices on supermarket and library bulletin boards, and by performing an Internet search for play groups and your town's name. Don't take it personally if you find an existing group but the organizers are not taking new members. Many play groups choose to limit membership.

Here are some tips to ease the transition into an existing group:

- Be respectful of the existing structure and rules of the group.

- Especially when you first join, arrive early at the play group to let your child have a few minutes to get settled before all the children arrive.

- Don't push for changes in the group until you have been an active member for a few months.

- Try to set up some one-on-one play dates with group members so that you and your child become more familiar with other parents and kids.

- Even if it's not your turn to host the play group, offer to help. It's an opportunity for the adults to get to know each other.

Not for Moms Only: Dad-Run Play Groups

There's no reason why dads can't organize and run play groups for their children. Check local community bulletin boards or perform an Internet search to discover local dad-run groups. Often, stay-at-home dads organize groups for the same social reason that motivates moms: a desire to meet other fathers in the community. A stay-at-home dad shouldn't hesitate, however, to join a primarily mother-run group. The goal is to provide a fun, safe experience for your child.

The Least You Need to Know

- Reach out to your community through word of mouth and advertising to find other parents interested in organizing a play group.

- Parents need to be honest with prospective members about their needs and expectations for a play group.

- Adequate adult supervision during the play group session is critical for the safety of all children.

- Children thrive on a consistent schedule and that the length of the sessions should be tied to the youngsters' developmental maturity.

- Fathers may organize their own play groups or choose to join one primarily run by mothers.

Chapter

3

Opening Day

In This Chapter

- Organizing the house and toys before play group participants arrive
- Sharing and other social skills
- Developing a schedule of activities for the play group
- What to bring to play group
- Tips for dealing with separation anxiety
- Super snacks for hungry kids (and parents)

Now that you have the most important component of a play group—members—you're ready to plan opening day! Organization simplifies the process and ensures that everyone—parents and kids—has a good time.

You'll want to have a structure and rhythm to play group sessions. Children thrive on routine. But you also need to be flexible. If the weather conspires against your planned outdoor activity, be prepared with something fun to do indoors. If all the kids are starting to get tired and cranky, settle down with a good story or some music—even if it's not story time yet. (In Chapters 8 and 9, we offer a host of indoor and outdoor activities sure to excite and engage the children.)

You also want to prepare your child for participating in the play group. She may need help sharing her toys with other children when it's your family's turn to host the group. She may have some separation anxiety if you're planning on leaving her. She may also become shy and unwilling to interact with the adults or other children. In this chapter, you'll find suggestions to ease your child's transition into a play group environment.

Getting Your House Ready for Play Group

Besides childproofing the room(s) or outdoor space you will use when you host the play group (see Chapter 4), consider how you will organize the space. You need to have room for the children—and at least in the beginning, for all the parents. Here are some tips:

- If you have a child-size table and chairs, bring them into the play group room for snack time.

- Remove all breakable objects and cover any furniture with drop cloths if you're concerned about stains.

- If you're going to use the dining room or kitchen table for art projects, cover it with a plastic cloth. Lay out the art supplies before the group arrives.

- Organize toys by type in different sections of the room so that children can spread out.

- If parents are going to stay in another room, have enough chairs and snacks available.

- Set up a changing area with diapers, baby wipes, diaper cream, plastic bags for disposal or a covered diaper pail, and so on in the playroom so that if someone needs to change a diaper, he or she doesn't have to leave the room. It's safer, although not as easy on your back, to change the child on the floor so that there's no chance of leaving a child unattended on a changing table. Although it's recommended that all families bring their own child's diapers (or pull-up diapers or underwear), have some available in case of emergency.

- Make sure that there's a bathroom nearby. When you take a child to the bathroom, there should always be another adult who remains with the other children. Make sure that children use soap and water to clean their hands after using the potty.

Preparing Your Child for Hosting a Play Group

Before it's your family's turn to host the play group, you need to talk to your child about the concept of sharing. While he probably has had other experiences sharing his toys, this may be different. The scenario involves more than one child, and they're coming to his home.

Go through the playroom with him and have him decide which toys need to be put away during play group. Certainly remove any that are not age appropriate (if you have older children) and any that cannot be replaced. Favorite stuffed animals or dolls should also be put away until after play group. Review with him the rule that if a toy is in the playroom, all children may play with it. Reassure him that the toys will not leave with the children.

ABC Play Group Chatter

Sharing was always a problem. I tried to make it a game. Before groups at my house, my oldest son and I used to put away all the green toys because, for some reason, he couldn't bear to share those. I've no idea why. My daughter made me put away special dolls. This was a good way to ensure that they knew they had to share everything else.

—Betsy, mother of four

Review the play group program with him and have him help you plan the activities. Let him be the host: showing children where to put their coats and boots when they come in, bringing them into the playroom, and picking out the book(s) that will be read to the group during story time. If you're not having a cooking activity, let him choose the snack and distribute it to the children at the table. These are important social skills he will learn.

Toys, Toys, Toys

You want to offer the play group a variety of toys so that the youngsters have options during free play. Avoid gender stereotypes: expect girls to play with trucks and boys to play with dolls.

To reduce squabbling, offer duplicates of the same kind of toy—such as a "fleet" of trucks, plenty of Legos, and enough dolls and stuffed animals so that every child can carry one. You don't have to take out every toy your child owns, but you do want the kids to have choices (deciding what you want to play with is a learning experience itself).

Play Group Do's

Look for fat crayons and markers. These are easier for young children to grasp.

Be realistic about your space. If you have small riding toys, can they be used if there are several children in the room? It's one thing if your child is scooting around the playroom when she's home alone, but it's another when a youngster is roaming around in a play car and there are other children in the room. If it's a danger, remove the riding toys and save them for outdoor play.

Play Group Do's

In 2007, more than a million toys were recalled by manufacturers because they were painted with lead paint. Even small amounts of lead are dangerous to children. You can't tell by looking at a toy whether it contains lead. There are home tests for lead content, but they're not 100 percent reliable. Check the Consumer Product Safety Commission's website, www.cpsc.gov, for a current list of product recalls. Have your own child's blood tested for lead annually. You can also sign up for free recall and safety news from the Consumer Product Safety Commission at www.cpsc.gov/cpsclist.aspx.

Now What Do We Do?

Members can decide to make the play group session as structured or as open-ended as they prefer. You can opt to have essentially one large free-play session for the kids, with no planned activities.

On the other hand, it enriches the experience and reduces the potential for squabbling if there's a plan for the day. And, as I've mentioned, kids thrive on routine.

Here's a suggested schedule for a play group session of two hours, starting at 9:30 A.M. and running until 11:30 A.M.:

9:30–9:50	Arrival and free play; toys are out on the floor and art supplies are on the table
9:50–10:10	Circle time, which can be a story, music, dance, finger play, a group art project, or a group baking project
10:10–10:30	Outdoor play, which can include a jungle gym, riding vehicles, a sandbox, and nature exploration
10:30–10:45	Snack time, which includes preparation, distribution, and cleanup
10:45–11:10	Free play
11:10–11:30	Cleanup followed by story time and departure

For younger children, you may want to shorten the play group session to 90 minutes. Reduce the time for each activity or maybe eliminate some. For example, for babies and toddlers it's probably wiser to stay indoors for the entire session—unless all parents are staying for play group and are responsible for getting their children dressed and ready for outdoor play.

For older children who can put on their own coats (even if they need help with mittens, boots, zippers, and so on), allow extra time to get them outdoors and back inside again.

Diaper Bag/Backpack Essentials

Each time you bring your child to a play group, you should pack a diaper bag or backpack with the following essentials. (Remember to update the clothes in the backpack throughout the year to account for your child's growth and the change in seasons.) You want to be prepared for your child to participate fully in all activities.

- Change(s) of underwear. For children in diapers, bring at least one diaper for every hour you're away from home. It's unlikely you'll need them all, but better safe than sorry. For children who are being toilet trained, bring several pull-up diapers. Even for those who are completely toilet trained, bring a change of underwear just in case.
- Baby wipes
- Diaper cream if you use it
- Complete change of clothes, including socks
- Smock for art projects (can be an old adult-sized shirt)
- Plastic bags to dispose of soiled diapers and to bring home soiled clothes

Teddy Bears, Blankets, and Pacifiers

Young children frequently have security objects such as stuffed animals, blankets, or pacifiers. These offer a child a safe haven when they are stressed. Regrettably, you may be the focus of uninvited comments about your child's need for one of these objects. Take comfort that nobody goes off to college with a pacifier. A toddler doesn't care what other people think about his need for his blanket or stuffed doggie—and neither should you. Your child will give it up when he's ready, although you may be able to help him through the transition.

Starting play group, although it sounds like lots of fun (and will be), can still be stressful for a little kid. If your child needs to bring a "lovey" with her, agree that it can come in the car but must stay in her backpack during play group. You don't want other children trying to play with this special object. This way, your child has the security of having her "lovey" nearby without any squabbles over who can hold it.

Follow this basic rule of thumb: if it's at play group, then any child can play with it. If you don't want others to touch it, don't put it out.

Separation Anxiety

By definition, a play group is supposed to be fun for parents and children. It's not jail, and nobody has to belong to a play group. If your play group has agreed that only the parents on duty that week have to stay, you may welcome the opportunity of a few free hours. But leaving your unhappy child at play group may not be worth it. So, no matter what other parents are doing, you have to follow your own instincts about what your child needs. It may well be that you are the only parent who has to stay with her child each and every time. That's okay. It's what he needs right now.

You may wonder what's provoking this anxiety about separation. Generally speaking, separation anxiety doesn't signify any significant emotional issue or problem. It's hard on the parent, but it's developmentally appropriate—and it too will pass.

Some children have no problems separating from their parents. It's not a reflection on their family relationships, either. If you have one of those kids, congratulations! You may not have a similar experience with the next one.

What Is Separation Anxiety?

You don't have to be a kid to experience separation anxiety. Think about how you feel when you enter a party and don't know a soul. Wouldn't you welcome a friendly face?

Play Group Do's

If your child is nervous about going to a play group, try to arrive slightly early so that he can get settled in before all the other children arrive.

Preschoolers have a strong attachment to their parents, and it's that attachment that is the foundation for healthy emotional development in adults. The loving relationship an infant has with his parents teaches him that the adult world can be counted on to provide him with his basic needs.

Just as a child learns, when she plays peekaboo, that her mother reappears from behind her hands, so a youngster discovers that separation is followed by reunion. But it may take her some time to realize that.

Who's at Risk?

Some children are more prone to separation anxiety than others. Separation is about change, and if your child has trouble adapting to new things, he may make more of a fuss when it comes to starting a play group. Consider the following questions:

- How does he react to a new babysitter?
- Does he readily try new foods?
- Does he need the exact same routine every night at bedtime?
- Is he normally shy around other children and adults?

This child will eventually adapt to play group, preschool, regular school, and even college—but it may take a little more patience and reassurance. Other kids seem to embrace change and are more flexible about new things. It's not good or bad; it's just different.

Play Group Don'ts

Don't be afraid of a crying child. It's easier to deal with a child who is open about his emotions and expresses his unhappiness and fears. More troubling is the child who retreats and is quiet and withdrawn. That child's fears may be overlooked.

The younger the child, the more likely you'll see strong separation anxiety. Infants typically start to experience problems with separating from their parents around nine months. For some kids, it's more acute than others, and it eases over time. As the youngster turns three and four, she's had more opportunities to experience her parents leaving and then returning. She has learned it isn't permanent. Remember, too, that if you have a child who has a "late birthday"—if he is one of the youngest in the group—he may have a more difficult time adjusting than the "older" children in the group.

Look out, too, for changes at home that are reflected in increased anxiety. A new baby in the house, a grandparent's illness, moving, parents separating—any of these life changes may increase a child's difficulty with separation. Sometimes a child will have problems with a parent leaving if the youngster hasn't been at play group for a few weeks. It's like he's starting over again. The bottom line is a need for parental patience.

Solutions to the Problem

Because separation anxiety is normal and will often pass as the child becomes comfortable in the new setting, the first solution is to wait it out. Don't insist that your child be on the same timetable for separating as other children in the group.

The question becomes whether the other parents will be troubled by your decision to stay at every play group session. Will they pressure you because they are afraid that their own children will insist upon them staying if you do? Talk about peer pressure! You need to do what's right for your child and not let the opinions of the other parents force you into leaving if your child isn't ready.

Play Group Do's

Take it day by day when trying to separate from your child. There will be steady progress, but there may also be steps backward. Patience is the key.

On the other hand, you should continue to try and help your child deal with his anxiety and separate successfully from you. Here are some tips:

- **Step by step works best.** Separating from your child may require a series of incremental steps. The first few play group sessions may find you literally by his side. Gradually, you may be able to move away from your child while still staying within eyesight in the same room. The next step might be for you to move into an adjacent room, out of sight but easily within reach. Finally, you may be able to leave.

- **Patience is key.** If your child is having a hard time separating from you, you must remain patient even when it appears that every other child seems much more independent than yours.

- **Say goodbye.** Although it's tempting to slip out unnoticed while your child is engaged, that breaks a sacred trust. Your child has to know that if you say you're in the next room, that is exactly where he will find you if he goes looking.

- **Use child-friendly terms.** If you do leave, explain when you will return in language your child can understand. For example, you might tell him that you will be back for snack time. That's easier for him to understand than telling him you'll be back in an hour. If he understands the rhythm of the play group, he'll know that you will return after he has played outdoors and has come in for the group's snack.

- **Never ridicule his anxiety.** Comments like, "Only babies cry" are hurtful and counterproductive.

- **No comparisons are allowed.** Don't compare his behavior to others in the group. Your child can't help his anxieties, and you wouldn't want him comparing your behavior to the other parents, either.

- **Establish a routine for separating.** Develop a ritual for leaving. For example, one mother used to say, "See you later, alligator." The little girl would answer, "After while, crocodile." It's an old joke, but it was their own little secret. Whatever works for your child, repeat it.

Is It Ever Okay to Leave a Crying Child at Play Group?

There are really several relationships that are affected when you leave your child at play group when she is obviously upset. First is the parent-child connection. Second, but equally important, is the relationship of the parent/caregiver to the other adult members of the group. Are they willing to help you by offering your child additional support in your absence? Third, and also important, is the relationship of the child with the other children in the group. If your child is very upset during play group because you have left, will the care of the other children be affected? Will they be able to do all the planned activities if one of the adults on duty has to care for your child?

You know your child best of all. Trust your judgment. You know whether she will quiet down after a few moments and begin to play or whether she will continue to be upset and disengaged from the group. Here's a step-by-step guide to help your child adjust to separation:

1. Don't rush to leave. Let your child become adjusted to play group—to both adults and children. This may take several weeks of you remaining in the room with her. You may move from being right by her side to gradually being in the room but across from her while she plays.

2. Gradually move from the room in which the children are playing to an adjacent room where you are still readily accessible.

3. If you believe that your child will only be momentarily upset—but, with the support of the adults on duty, will then be reassured enough to join the activities of the group—try to leave. But take a cell phone or pager with you so that you are reachable if it's necessary, and only leave if the adults in the group will support you.

Praise your child at each step. Being able to leave isn't just to give you a few hours of free time. It will build her self-esteem and confidence if your child can successfully stay at play group by herself.

ABC Play Group Chatter

It's a big world out there. Some kids jump right in, and some need to test the water with their toes before they're comfortable wading in. (And then they wade very slowly, of course!) Be patient. With some gentle guidance your child will leave your side.

—Elizabeth Pantley, *Perfect Parenting: The Dictionary of 1,000 Parenting Tips*

What If It's Not Working?

If your child continues to cry or refuses to engage in the activities—and this behavior has gone on for several weeks—it's time to reassess whether this play group is right for your child. You have several options:

- If he enjoys the play group when you remain with him, then it may be worthwhile to continue with the group (assuming the other members agree) and simply stay during each session. Eventually, your child may mature enough to be able to separate—not on other children's timetables, but on his own.

- It may not be a good match and you should quit the group. Your child may not be comfortable with the children or the adults. Yes, he is a child, but you need to respect his feelings. When you look at the situation objectively, can you see what it is that is frightening him? Or are there other things happening in your family's life (divorce, death, a move) that are stressful? Perhaps this isn't the best time to try and force the issue.

- Does your child just need a little more time to develop? Perhaps a younger play group would be better. Forget his chronological age; would your child fare better with younger children? Perhaps the children in the group are more mature than he is, and putting him with children who are a few months younger would be less stressful.

Keep in mind that this is a volunteer group of parents, not trained young childhood education professionals. Make sure that you are comfortable with the way the other adults in the group will support your child if she is having difficulty. Will they be loving, caring, reassuring? Is she the only child who is upset, or are there several kids having a hard time? If that's the case, the group should reassess whether it's wise to permit any adults to leave and ask all parents/caregivers to stay during play group.

Healthy, Fun Snacks

For kids (and probably many adults), snack time is one of the highlights of the day. Especially in play group and school settings, it's much more than just an opportunity to eat. In Chapter 10, I review the educational components of snack time.

But beyond any math lessons that are learned as kids distribute the napkins, juice glasses, and individual snacks, there is also a wealth of social skills that are being practiced as the children figuratively or literally "break bread." Snack time feeds the stomach, but also the soul. It's an opportunity for children to socialize with each other.

Assuming you are providing healthy snacks, snack time is an important part of a preschooler's diet. Young children need to eat more frequently because their stomachs are smaller and can't hold as much at one time as adults. Furthermore, all that activity is burning up calories.

ABC Play Group Chatter

According to Karen M. Chapman-Novakofski, professor of nutrition at the University of Illinois, "Preschoolers need about 1,200 calories per day. If their activity level is moderate to high, they should probably take in even more calories. Snacks provide an estimated 20 to 25 percent of a preschooler's total energy intake."

Play group members should agree on what is considered a healthy snack. Generally, provide a drink (water, milk, or unsugared juice—avoid soda) and kid-friendly food such as graham crackers, cheese cut into very small cubes, or diced fruit with yogurt. Little ones can easily choke on nuts, seeds, popcorn, grapes, and hot dogs. All food should be cut into small, easily chewed finger foods. Watch all children closely when they are eating.

You need to make the group "peanut free" if any of the children have a peanut allergy. As a general rule, children younger than age one shouldn't be offered peanut butter, and if one of the parents has a peanut allergy, they shouldn't offer peanut butter to their child—if at all—until the child is at least three years old. Note any allergies your child has on the Emergency Medical Release Form (see Chapter 4).

Play Group Do's

Plan a cooking activity with the children. They can help prepare their snack. "Ants on a Log" is a fun project, and depending on a child's fine motor control, it can be done entirely or in part by the youngster. Fill celery stalks cut about three inches long with cream cheese. Sprinkle raisins along the spread to make "ants."

The Least You Need to Know

- Get your house ready for play group by doing a safety check and deciding, before the children arrive, what toys you will provide and which you will put away.

- Prepare your child for play group, and let him serve as the host.

- Organize your child's backpack for play group to include a change of clothing, diapers if needed, and an art smock.

- Separation anxiety is normal and takes patience, comfort, and empathy to resolve.

- If your child continues to be unhappy in a play group, it may be wise to quit the group or look for a more compatible one.

- Snack time is an important element of the play group session, providing needed nutrition for children and the opportunity to practice social skills.

4

For Your Child's Health and Safety

In This Chapter

- Childproofing strategies inside and out
- In case of emergency …
- Vaccination requirements and allergy alerts
- Illness rules for the group
- When caregivers are sick

Keeping your child healthy and safe is your paramount concern. You want to be sure that the play group location has been adequately childproofed. If your group takes turns meeting at members' homes, then you must develop a checklist of basic safety standards.

Parents also need to make explicit rules about health issues. You want to be clear about when you expect a parent to keep a child at home because of illness. You need to develop a notification system if a child has a communicable illness or condition and the play group members have been exposed.

You may also want to discuss the issue of vaccinations. Do you want to require all children in the play group to have been immunized against common childhood diseases? Members will also want to discuss how to handle emergencies that arise during play group time.

Safety First

Wherever your play group meets, you want to be sure that it's appropriately childproofed. If it's a public facility, such as a room in a church or library, appoint one member to be responsible for bringing appropriate childproofing equipment each time (electrical outlet covers, for example). If you meet in a private home, agree on the safety standards for both indoor and outdoor play areas.

Play Group Do's

Make sure each home has a fully functional fire extinguisher. Know where it's kept and how to use it.

Indoor Safety

Childproofing requires you to look at a space from a child's point of view. Literally, get down on your hands and knees and look around the room to see potential dangers. Don't assume that because adults will be in the room, the kids will be safe. Make the room safe, *and* always have adults present. Here are some indoor childproofing tips:

- **Pets.** Put all animals behind locked doors, even if you know that your pet is harmless.

- **Electrical.** Make sure to cover all electrical outlets. Wrap and tuck away in plastic tubing all electrical cords and wires. If necessary, check and replace any frayed electrical cords.

- **Furniture.** Check that tall pieces of furniture, such as bookcases or a dresser, are stable and preferably securely attached to the wall. If you can't secure a piece, then block off access to it. You don't want a child pulling the furniture over. Put corner guards on furniture with sharp edges (coffee and end tables, for example). Move any tables with glass tops out of children's reach.

- **Fireplaces.** Do not light a fire while play group is in session, and don't use the room if the fireplace is still hot. Clean the fireplace if it was used recently, and remove all ashes. Put fireplace tools out of reach.

- **Plants.** Keep out of reach of children. Some plants are poisonous. It's just safer to keep all plants out of reach as well as any fertilizer, bug spray, and gardening tools.

- **Cabinets and drawers.** Use childproof locks on cabinets and drawers that contain anything dangerous (knives, for example) or anything fragile. Lock up any possessions that you don't want children to touch.

- **Cleaning products.** Lock away all cleaning products.

- **Medicines.** Lock away all prescription and over-the-counter drugs as well as cosmetics.

- **Doors.** Either lock or put doorknob covers on exterior doors as well as on the doors to rooms you want to make off limits. Also, check the doorstops in the rooms you use. Some have a rubber tip that's removable, creating a potential choking hazard. Remove it permanently.

- **Windows.** Put bars or devices on windows to prevent them from fully opening. Tie up, out of a child's reach, all cords for window blinds. Make sure that there are no loops in the cords.

- **Oven.** Add an oven guard and stove lock to protect the children from an overheated oven door, potential burns, and gas leaks.

ABC Play Group Chatter

Since 1991, the United States Consumer Product Safety Commission has tracked more than 169 strangulation deaths caused by window coverings. Most were children ages three and younger.

- **Stairs.** Put gates at the top and bottom of all stairs to prevent children from going up or down by themselves.

- **Trash cans.** Cover and put away all trash cans.

Outdoor Safety

If the play group meets outside, you may want to have additional adults on duty. Here are some outdoor childproofing tips:

- **Yard.** If possible, meet in a fenced-in area. But don't use the fact that it's a confined space to reduce adult vigilance.

- **Sandbox.** Put corner guards on any sharp edges. Make sure the sandbox is covered when not in use to prevent the deposit of animal waste products.

- **Playground equipment.** Make sure that the equipment is scaled for young children (in other words, no more than five feet high). There should be a protective surface below and a six- to eight-foot perimeter surrounding the equipment so that a child can descend safely without falling onto another child or structure. Any platform or walkway more than 20 inches above the ground should have guardrails or protective barriers. Run your fingers over wooden equipment to make sure that there are no rough edges, splinters, or loose screws.

ABC Play Group Chatter

According to the United States Consumer Product Safety Commission, more than 100,000 injuries occur annually on public playgrounds. Children age 10 and younger suffer 80 percent of these injuries.

- **Under-equipment surface.** Neither grass nor cement is a forgiving surface. You want the surface under playground equipment to be impact absorbing. Wood mulch, pea gravel, and sand are good surfaces if they are properly maintained. The material should be at least 9 to 12 inches deep, which means that the material will need to be replenished as needed. Synthetic, foam-like tiles or rubber mats made especially for playground use are also good.

- **Pools.** If the home has a pool, make sure it's fenced off with a lock on the gate. Make sure that all wading pools are empty during play group. Water is fun, but it's also a hazard. Avoid pool play during play group even if you have extra adults on duty.

$A\mathcal{B}C$ **Play Group Chatter**

> According to the National Safety Council, drowning claims the lives of nearly 3,000 people every year. Children four years old and younger have the highest death rate due to drowning.

Emergency Care

The play group needs to be prepared for a worst-case scenario. What if a child falls ill or is injured, the parent or caregiver cannot be reached, and immediate medical care is needed? To handle this "what-if" situation, every family should complete and sign an emergency medical release form. The play group organizer should maintain a file of these papers, and each family (or guardian) should also keep a copy of the form in the child's diaper bag/backpack. The following sample form gives you the basic information that is needed. You might want to make several copies of this blank form to have on hand.

Emergency Medical Release Form

Child: _____

Date of Birth: _____

Parent or Guardian: _____

Family Physician: _____

    Phone: _____

    Address: _____

    _____

Hospital Preference: _____

In case of emergency, if family physician cannot be reached, I hereby authorize my child to be treated by Certified Emergency Personnel (i.e., EMT, First Responder, E.R. Physician).

In case of emergency, contact (it's a good idea to have at least two names for emergency contact):

    Name: _____

    Phone: _____

    Relationship to child: _____

Please list any allergies/medical problems, including those requiring maintenance medication (i.e., diabetes, asthma, seizure disorder), to ensure that medical personnel have details of any medical problem that may interfere with or alter treatment:

Medical Diagnosis	Medication	Dosage	Frequency of Dosage

Date of last Tetanus Toxoid Booster: _____

Authorized Parent/Guardian Signature:

_____

Date: _____

Wherever the play group meets, be sure to have a fully stocked first-aid kit on hand. Here are the items that should be included:

- First-aid manual
- Sterile gauze
- Adhesive tape
- Adhesive bandages in several sizes
- Elastic bandage
- Antiseptic wipes
- Soap
- Antibiotic cream
- Antiseptic solution (such as hydrogen peroxide)
- Hydrocortisone cream (over-the-counter strength)
- Acetaminophen (no aspirin)
- Tweezers
- Sharp scissors
- Disposable instant cold packs
- Alcohol wipes
- Thermometer
- Plastic gloves
- Mouthpiece for administering CPR
- Flashlight and extra batteries

Along with the first-aid kit, keep the following information handy for each child:

- Emergency contact information
- Important health information such as any food or drug allergies
- The phone number for the child's pediatrician
- The phone number for the local children's hospital
- The phone number for the American Association of Poison Control Centers' national emergency hotline: 1-800-222-1222
- The phone numbers of local police, fire, and rescue squads

Store the kit out of reach of children but somewhere easily accessible by adults.

Play Group Do's

If you're meeting in a public facility rather than a private home, make sure that there's a phone on the premises (either a landline or cell phone). Post the address of the meeting place next to the phone. In the event of an emergency, it's easy to forget the address when under stress.

Vaccination Issues

Whether or not parents choose to have their child vaccinated is a personal medical decision. In this book, we don't review the pros and cons of vaccinating against childhood diseases. It's reasonable, however, to ask members to disclose their child's immunization history to the group. You don't want to invade anyone's privacy; rather, you want to make sure that other members aren't put at risk. For example, a family decides not to vaccinate their child for rubella. Here's the problem. If the unvaccinated youngster contracts the disease, he might pass it on to a pregnant woman who is a member of the group. As a result, the fetus is at increased risk of being born with birth defects.

You can find the current immunization schedule for children ages zero to six years, recommended by the Centers for Disease Control (CDC), at www.cdc. gov/vaccines/recs/schedules/default.htm.

Allergy Alert

If a child in the group has a food, bee, or other allergy, make sure that all members are aware of the condition. Families must also provide instructions for emergency care should the child be exposed to the allergen. Some children are so allergic that they can suffer an anaphylactic reaction (which is life-threatening). If the family's doctor has prescribed an EpiPen for treatment upon exposure, make sure that all adult members of the play group are instructed how to administer the treatment. Be sure to alert any new members of the group (if a new caregiver for a family is now attending the play group sessions, for example).

If a child has a severe peanut allergy that can be triggered simply by being near peanuts, you should make the play group sessions nut-free. This means that the group cannot serve *any* peanut products at all.

ABC Play Group Chatter

The number of children with peanut allergies has doubled, according to a survey reported in *Journal of Allergy and Clinical Immunology*.

Kids Get Sick

Some children seem to catch one thing after another. Sometimes colds appear to last from September to May. The truth is that you develop immunity to a virus by contracting the virus (or being immunized against it). Kids get sick a lot because they haven't developed enough immunities yet.

There are more than 100 cold viruses (rhinoviruses)—and sometimes it seems like your child is determined to contract each one. The ear infections that seem to accompany many colds are the result of fluid buildup in the middle ear, which occurs because ears in young children often don't drain efficiently (a self-correcting condition as they grow older). There are also more than 60 strains of enteroviruses, which cause diarrhea and vomiting.

Play Group Do's

The play group's diaper changing pad should be cleaned and disinfected (or changed) after every diaper change. Wipe it down with antibacterial wipes.

Being in a play group increases a child's exposure to germs and viruses. In many ways, that's a good thing because most common childhood illnesses are fairly mild when contracted by a child. These same diseases, if contracted by an adult, can be more painful and result in more complications. You want your child's immune system to develop. It's just that you need to be realistic about the likelihood that your child is now going to catch more colds and other childhood diseases.

In a play group, transmission of germs is easy. The room may be overheated and crowded. The kids cluster together. Viruses are transmitted whenever a preschooler touches an infected child (or a discarded tissue), then touches his own nose or mouth. Cold viruses can live for several hours on countertops and toys.

The simplest way to reduce the transmission of disease is to insist that kids and adults wash their hands with soap. This reduces the transmission of germs from other people, from surfaces, and from animals. According to a study reported in the medical journal *Lancet*, children who wash their hands with soap reduce their chances of getting diarrhea or pneumonia by 50 percent.

Play Group Do's

Teach your child to cover his nose and mouth when he sneezes or coughs and then to wash his hands with soap and water immediately afterward.

When to Keep Your Child Home

The fear is that your child will be sick for the entire winter and will never be able to come to play group. Here are the general guidelines regarding when to keep your child at home, but check with your doctor for guiding principles for your family:

- **Fever.** If your child has a fever, she should stay home until her temperature has been normal for 24 hours.

- **Antibiotics.** If your child is on antibiotics, keep her at home for at least the first 24 hours she is on the medication.

- **Pink or running eyes.** Keep her at home until you get a definite diagnosis from your doctor about the cause.

- **Undiagnosed rash.** Keep her at home until the rash clears up or you get a firm diagnosis from the doctor and are told that the rash is not contagious.

- **Diarrhea/vomiting.** Keep your child at home until these conditions have stopped.

Other signs of illness are irritability, lethargy, persistent crying, or difficulty breathing. Keep your child at home and consult your doctor if you are concerned.

Don't "drop and run." That's where a parent knowingly drops off a sick child at play group and rushes out without explanation. Even if you think your youngster only has a little fever and isn't contagious, it's not fair to other families or to your child. Trust your gut instinct: if you think your child is ill, then keep her home.

When Parents/Caregivers Are Sick

Working with kids can be hazardous to your health. In one 1997–1998 study by the Occupational Safety and Health Administration (OSHA), daycare workers suffered nearly 12,000 on-the-job injuries. Just as kids catch colds and other illnesses from their playmates, the adults in the group are also being exposed to these same viruses and germs. Plus, there are the risks of sprains and back injuries from picking up kids, chasing after them, or tripping and falling over the toys spread out everywhere!

Obviously, the same rules of conduct (see earlier in the chapter) for when to keep your child at home because of illness apply to adults, as well. If you're sick, you shouldn't be attending play group and exposing others to your germs. If it's your turn to be one of the adults on duty—or if it's your turn to host the play group at your home—make arrangements to trade off.

But should your child attend without you? Yes, assuming that she doesn't have a fever or any of the other symptoms that would preclude attendance. It also assumes that your child will be comfortable attending play group without you. If she is likely to remain unhappy throughout the entire session, don't insist that she attend. It only puts a burden on other group members to try and comfort your child while providing adequate supervision for other kids.

The Least You Need to Know

- Wherever the play group meets, make sure that indoor and outdoor play spaces are childproofed.

- Keep a well-stocked first-aid kit handy during all play group meetings, and have readily available the Emergency Medical Release Form for each child.

- Discuss the immunization status and any allergy concerns of all children in the play group.

- Establish clear rules for when children and adults are considered too sick to attend play group.

Chapter 5

Little Kids, Big Problems

In This Chapter

- The widespread problem of bullying
- Helping engage a shy child
- What's mine is yours
- Hurtful cliques
- Aggressive behavior
- Developmental differences in children

This chapter deals with a range of child-focused issues, including aggression, shyness, cliques, and different rates of maturation among kids. These issues may impact how well the group interacts. They may be little kids, but they often have big problems. But with planning and patience, you may be able to resolve or ameliorate the concerns.

Bullying

Fifty percent of children and teens experience bullying at some point in their lives. One in five experience bullying on a regular basis. Not surprisingly, some bullies start at a young age. Bullying isn't limited to physical abuse such as biting, hitting, and kicking. Verbal and emotional abuse, including teasing, are just as destructive. The newest kind of bullying is done online. As children spend so much time on the Internet, be alert to cyberbullying when your child is school-age.

Bullying victims tend to be younger, weaker, and more passive. Size has nothing to do with it. One mother recalls her three-year-old daughter's constant complaints about a boy who was always aggressive at the playground. When the mother investigated, she saw that the boy was very small for his age. Her daughter probably outweighed him by 10 pounds. But his demeanor was much more belligerent than her quieter daughter.

Why Do Children Bully?

Some bullying is a result of deep-seated psychological issues relating to family and living circumstances. These situations require professional intervention.

Some bullying is less extreme, although it still needs to be addressed. Sometimes a child acts out because he is feeling insecure or has low self-esteem. Sometimes he bullies because there has been a significant change at home, such as his parents' divorce or a new baby in the house. Bullying is a way of trying to exert control over his life.

Dealing with a Bully

If you observe bullying in the play group, the first action is to stop it. But be sure to observe the situation carefully. Remember that there is a difference between a fair fight and a bullying incident. A fair fight is where each child is using his words, not his fists, to express his point of view. It's not bullying just because one child may be louder than the other. If both children are holding their own, it's worth it to see whether they can work it out themselves.

If you intervene in a fair fight, try to give them the tools and framework to resolve the difference by themselves. For example, if both want to play with a truck, ask for their ideas on how to solve the conflict. Help them brainstorm resolutions. For example, they could take turns; they could get other vehicles and build a fleet; or together they could build a roadway with blocks and then "drive" the truck down the streets.

Sometimes kids tease each other in a good-natured way and both laugh about it. Sometimes if one child's feelings get hurt, you can see that it's a singular incident—not a consistent reflection of the relationship.

Bullying is different. Bullying is when one child is being intimidated by another. When the interaction between the children is unequal and unfair, that kind of behavior should not be tolerated.

Shyness

It's always best to avoid labeling a child. It can become a self-fulfilling prophecy. Parents are often concerned that their child is shy, yet about 30 to 40 percent of adults consider themselves shy. Some research suggests that shyness may be inherited. Experts have found that most shy children have at least one parent who is also shy.

What you want is for your child to feel comfortable with herself. Her temperament is different than the child who is naturally outgoing and at ease among strangers. But different is not good or bad; it's just different. What's important is that you don't want your child's shyness to keep her from participating in fun activities.

Experts consider childhood shyness normal if:

- In new situations and among strangers, given enough time and patience, the child relaxes and engages.
- The child is able to relax and engage in small groups, even if large groups intimidate him.
- The child is able to make friends.

If you are concerned that your child's shyness is stopping him from enjoying new and fun experiences, talk to your doctor.

ABC Play Group Chatter

> We had one little girl who was very shy and withdrawn and often "didn't listen"… until it was discovered that the child had hearing issues. We did share concerns with the mom, who shared concerns with her pediatrician.
>
> —Wendy, mother of two

Here are some suggestions to help your shy child make the transition to play group:

- Talk to your child about his fears and validate them. Let him know that you respect him and his temperament.

- Never label your child as shy.

- Prepare your child for any new experience. Talk through what will happen, and let him role play ways to handle the situation.

- Offer to host the play group at your house more often in the beginning so that he is in familiar surroundings.

- Be prepared to stay at play group longer than other parents to let your child become more comfortable with the other children and adults.

- Offer positive feedback when your child tries a new experience—even if he struggles and needs your help. Praise him for the effort.

Sharing

It sometimes seems like the first word a child learns is "mine." Tying for first place is "no." Combined, they pretty much sum up a preschooler's approach to sharing. "It's mine—and no, you can't have it."

Sharing is a learned art. Some kids are more easy-going than others. They may have an easier time sharing. But all kids have moments when sharing their toys is the last thing they want to do.

Toddlers think that ceding possession of a toy means giving it up forever. They don't understand the concept that it will be returned. You can force the issue, but maturation and patience resolve many sharing problems.

You want children to learn that sharing is a win-win proposition. If you share with another child, then the flip side is that the other child has to share with you. It's double the toy opportunities!

Here are some rules about sharing during play group:

- Before play group members arrive, put away any toy that you know is special to your child. She doesn't have to share everything.

- Ask your child which toys she is willing to share, then praise her when she makes the choices.

- Have similar types of toys available: multiple cars, dolls, and stuffed animals.

- Put out toys that invite sharing and cooperative play: blocks, Legos, tea sets, dress-up
  clothes, and so on.

- Reinforce with praise when you see your
  child (or another child in the play group)
  sharing nicely.

- Never belittle or call a child a baby for not
  sharing. If necessary, remove the toy from
  the play group so no one can play with it.

- If a toy is in demand, set a timer for five
  minutes. When it rings, give another child a
  turn.

Cliques

Cliques aren't just for teens. Unfortunately, you'll
find cliques even among preschoolers. Kids are
often very direct: "We're playing here, and you
can't play."

Excluding a child from group play is harmful to the
child who is left out as well as to the children in
control. You want to teach your child empathy—
the ability to understand how someone else feels.
Empathy, however, is a difficult concept for young
children to grasp. They are just beginning to
understand their own emotions.

Excluding for Cause

There are times when youngsters justifiably exclude
another child. If your child is routinely being

excluded, check to see whether her behavior might be part of the problem. Is she hitting, biting, kicking, or grabbing? Is she significantly younger or less mature than the other children?

If her actions are the issue, you must work with her to change the aggressive behavior. If it's a question of maturity, you may want to look for a play group with children who are at her developmental level (discussed later in the chapter). Don't focus on chronological age; children mature at different rates. Find her a play group that meets her immediate needs. If she outgrows those children, you can always change later on.

How to Help

If you believe that your child is being excluded because she's shy, help her develop one-on-one friendships with the play group children. Invite another child to your home for a one-on-one play date. As your child becomes more comfortable with the other children (and they with her), it's more likely that she'll be included.

On the other hand, if you see that certain children are routinely excluding other kids during play group—and that the group is becoming cliquish, with feelings being hurt—you will need to intervene. Try these suggestions:

- Set up activities where the children work together on a project.

- Have the excluded child help you with snack preparation or picking the book to read.
- Pair the child with a younger member of the play group so she can be the leader. You want to build her self-esteem and confidence.

Play Group Don'ts

Sometimes it's not only the children who have established a clique and are exclusive. You may notice that the parents of the cliquish kids seem to form a little clique themselves. If you find yourself in a play group where the parents aren't particularly welcoming or open to including someone new, find another group.

Aggression

Aggression in preschoolers can be the result of many things:

- A child may bite, kick, hit, scratch, pull hair, or grab because he is frustrated and doesn't have the verbal skills to express his emotions.
- He may act aggressively because he sees that behavior on television or in a computer game and thinks it's an acceptable way of acting.
- He may act out because of issues at home that have him confused, angry, or frustrated.

- He may act aggressively because he is a victim of that kind of behavior himself.

Regardless of the motivation behind the aggression, you need to stop the behavior immediately. Here are some tips:

- Remove the child who is acting aggressively from the group. Say clearly that biting, hitting, and so on is not acceptable.

- Have the aggressor sit down while you comfort the victim. Both children need attention. Remain calm.

- The aggressor may need a few moments to get his emotions under control. You may need to help him calm down. You aren't offering approval of his actions; rather, you're helping him get to the point where you can have a rational discussion.

- Remind the aggressor to use words. Help him verbalize his feelings: "I'm angry because …"

- Have the child apologize for his aggressive behavior. While he may not completely understand the words or may not necessarily be sincere in his apology, he will learn that he must take responsibility for bad behavior.

- Look for triggers to a child's aggressive behavior. Some situations can be avoided by planning ahead. For example, a youngster may lose control if he believes someone is playing with his favorite blanket or toy.

Removing that object from the play group may eliminate a trigger point.

- Offer outlets for aggressive behavior. For example, one mother set up a cartoon pop-up punching bag and had her frustrated son channel his aggression toward hitting the bag, not his little sister.

- You may need to play detective to decide whether there are some toxic friendships in the group. Does a certain child always act aggressively when playing with another youngster in the group? Can you see what is the trigger? Can you help him develop a stronger friendship with another child?

- No adult should ever hit, bite, kick, or act aggressively in order to "show the child what it's like."

- Offer praise for good behavior. Model the behavior you want the child to follow. Let him hear you use words, without yelling, when you are frustrated or angry.

Developmental Differences

The accepted wisdom is that boys mature more slowly than girls, but it's a little more complicated than that. It's probably more accurate to say that boys mature faster in some areas and slower in others than girls. A 1999 study by researchers at Virginia Tech University found that the areas of the brain involved in language and fine motor skills mature about six years earlier in girls than in boys, while the areas of the brain involved in targeting and spatial memory mature about four years earlier in boys than in girls. There are indeed physiological differences, but experts agree that gender differences are often reinforced by societal expectations of how boys and girls should act as well as the different ways adults interact with boys and girls.

Even more broadly, regardless of gender, there is a wide range of what is considered "normal" development. Some children walk before they are a year old; others are closer to 18 months before they take independent steps. One child may seem incredibly verbal—able to speak in complete sentences—while another may have a limited vocabulary.

It's helpful to remember that children develop at different rates, and it's likely you'll see some of these differences in your play group. These differences may impact the functioning of the group. A child with a limited vocabulary may express his frustration physically while another is able to use words to express his emotions. It's not to serve as an excuse for bad behavior but rather to provide adults with insight into the motivation. The bottom line, however, is that the bad behavior still has to be stopped. But with insight into motivation, adult response can be focused on helping the child develop his language.

Similarly, even if all the children are the same chronological age, developmental differences in the group may mean that activities have to be planned to take into account the range of abilities. It's also important not to fall into stereotypes of what activities should be planned for girls (dolls) and boys (blocks). Offer both sexes the same activities, and encourage all children to try new things.

One advantage of being in a play group is that it gives parents an opportunity to see the behavior and development of other children. Especially for first-time parents, it is a point of reference. If you are concerned that your child is not hitting developmental milestones as you see other children do, voice your concerns to your doctor.

The Least You Need to Know

- Bullying is unacceptable and can damage both the bully and the victim.

- When your shy child is about to encounter a new situation or people, build in enough time for her to adjust, relax, and feel comfortable.

- Help your child to understand that one of the advantages of sharing his toys at play group is that his friends will also share their toys with him.

- Even preschoolers can be cliquish, but excluding other youngsters from group play is hurtful.

- Aggression is sometimes a result of a child's inability to verbalize his emotions.

- Children develop at different rates, and you may need to tailor activities to meet different needs.

Chapter 6

Grown-Ups and Their Problems

In This Chapter

- A child-rearing competition?
- Handling conflicts in parenting styles
- Taking up the slack for other parents
- When the problem is someone else's child
- What to do if you suspect child abuse or domestic violence
- Quitting the play group on your own terms

How well the children in a play group interact is critical, but key to that success is also how well the adults in the group relate to each other. In this chapter, you'll find strategies for dealing with the hyper-competitive parent who is constantly setting up win-lose situations among the parents and kids. You'll also find ways to handle the parent who doesn't carry her share of the play group responsibilities as well as how to respond to differences in parenting styles. Partner abuse and child abuse are sensitive topics, but if you suspect either, here's what you must do. Finally, if the play group is not working for either the parent or the child, here's how to make a graceful exit.

The Competitive Parent

Some adults always need to be the best at everything, including having the "best" child. For these parents, like the old NASCAR saying goes, "finishing second is just finishing first among the losers." They always need to point out how their child is the smartest, most verbal, friendliest, and so on—and the implication (sometimes subtle, sometimes not) is that your child is not.

Sometimes the competition isn't just about the kids. This competitive parent drops names to impress and makes sure you know how successful she, her spouse, or her parents are. The competition can be verbal, or it can be a game of one-upsmanship. The child's birthday parties are over the top. Her food is strictly homemade or organic or whatever signifies "better." Weight, clothes, house—the competition can be about everything and nothing. It can even be a competition about who has the most problems, with the inference being her problems are meaningful and significant and yours are not.

A nickel psychoanalysis might suggest that insecurity is the motivation for the parent's boorish behavior. Whatever the reason, here are some tips for how to handle such a parent in play group:

- **Don't buy into her world.** Just because she declares authoritatively that her way is the best way, you don't have to accept it.

- **Separate friendship from play group.** It would be nice if every member of the play group became close friends, but sometimes it's enough if the kids have a pleasant outing. If the children are enjoying play group, ignore the boor and find other adults as friends.

- **Avoid the situation.** If this is a play group where parents take turns leaving, switch schedules so that you aren't on duty when she is.

- **Call her on her behavior.** If the competitive behavior is becoming intrusive or is affecting the children, you might try to tell the individual how you feel. Perhaps she isn't even aware of what she is doing. Be prepared for an angry or hurt response, but it may be worth it. You may have to decide whether the boorish parent's behavior is enough to make you question continuing in the group.

Conflicting Parenting Styles

One of the advantages of being in a play group is that you have the opportunity to observe different ways of handling parenting decisions. Sometimes it's a new, better way—and you've learned an effective technique for resolving a problem facing your family. Other times, you may be troubled by decisions another parent makes.

ABC **Play Group Chatter**

I quit a playgroup because there was a racist mom in the group who couldn't keep her feelings to herself. No matter what we talked about, somehow she found something bigoted to say about our topic of conversation. I wasn't about to get into an ethical discussion with this mom.

—Leah, mother of two

It's important that parents in the play group respect each other and accept that there will be differences in how they raise their children. There are two important caveats to that premise:

- Child abuse is never acceptable.
- No one can impose her views on another parent.

You may not agree with the "rules" in another family's home. Sometimes the rules may be minor; for example, the kids can eat in the living room, even if that's forbidden in your home. Sometimes it's a bigger issue; for example, the children may have pretend guns as toys, whereas you forbid them in your home.

Or, it can be even bigger issues—such as discipline. According to William Coleman, M.D., of the Center for Development and Learning at the University of North Carolina, Chapel Hill, and chair of the American Academy of Pediatrics (AAP) committee on psychosocial aspects of child and family health: "The AAP doesn't endorse spanking because it is not effective in the long term, can hurt a child's self-esteem, and can cause physical harm."

But there are families who do spank (and I'm making a clear distinction between spanking that is a swat on the bottom and abuse). You may indicate that you don't approve, but if it's not abusive, you may have to ignore it. You should certainly make clear that no one may ever spank your child. In fact, that's a rule that should be clear for all play groups. You should also discuss, among the adults, how you will handle when a child misbehaves in play group. Talk about how to effectively use time-outs. Agree on all the ground rules before you start a play group.

Here are some suggestions for how to handle differences in parenting style:

- **Talk to your child about how every family has its own rules, but in your family *this* is what is permitted.** Don't justify or apologize for the rules in your family. Explain clearly, "This is how we do it in our house."

- **Pick your battles.** You may have a distinctly different approach than another family, but how much does their choice impact you and your child? If it's minimal, or if it's a matter of simply disagreeing, then mutual respect says to let the situation pass. For example, you may not permit your child to watch certain television shows while another family doesn't have that rule. Even if the children discuss the show in play group, it may not be worth it to insist that all discussion be stopped. If your child presses you to let her watch the show based on play group discussions, you can certainly remind her of rule No. 1: "This is how we do it in our family."

- **Don't be afraid to speak up if you consider it an important issue.** If you believe there is a safety concern or that your child will be harmed, physically or emotionally, by a certain practice, say so. For example, if you know that another family owns guns, you should certainly demand to know where the guns are kept and the safety procedures they follow to protect the children from accessing the guns. If you feel strongly, you can also insist, for example, that play guns not be permitted during play group sessions. Even if the other family allows their children to play with pretend guns, you can ask that those toys be put away during play group.

- **You can intervene, but again, pick your battles.** For example, a child using bathroom humor is not unexpected among preschoolers, but you may have a smaller tolerance for it than the parent. It's reasonable to ask the child to stop, even if the parent is choosing to ignore it. You're in the room, and you can express your preferences. The parent may shrug it off or may be offended. You decide how much it bothers you, and it's reasonable to express your opinion.

- **With respect, raise differences for discussion.** It may be a learning opportunity for both parents and children. For example, around Easter time, would it bother you if, as an activity for the children, a parent planned for the kids to dye eggs? Would it make a difference if the parent planned the activity without considering that your family doesn't celebrate the holiday?

Rather than being angry, raise the concern and explain your viewpoint. You may ask that they not pursue that activity, or you may decide that it's harmless and that it will be an opportunity for you to talk to your child about your own family's beliefs. Either decision or any other you choose is appropriate if you have respect for differences. No proselytizing is permitted.

The Parent Who Shirks Responsibility or Is Unpleasant

Hopefully all members of the play group are willing to share the responsibilities of running the sessions. Unfortunately, often there is a parent who always has an excuse for why she can't take her turn, why she wasn't prepared with an activity, why she forgot a snack, or why she needs someone else to do her job.

ABC **Play Group Chatter**

We had one mom who would some-times "forget" to pick up her child, or at best, come late. We tolerated it for quite a while, knowing she was struggling with her husband, children, and life in general, until she left all our children at an activ-ity on her pickup day. One of the other moms, who had originally brought her into the group, told her that maybe this wasn't a great idea for her at this time. We con-nected her with a counselor at the local hospital.

—Wendy, mother of two

You've got a couple of choices if that's what's hap-pening in your play group:

● **Ignore it.** If the kids get along, the parent is pleasant (enough), and it's really no bur-den, you may choose to ignore her behavior. That's assuming that the children are always safe (even if bored) in her care. It may mean more work for the other members, but you may not think it's enough of a problem to take action.

- **Check to see whether there is an underlying problem.** There may be something happening in the parent's life that explains her behavior (for example, money worries, illness, marital issues, and so on). She may not have shared it with the group, but if it were known, everyone would be more than happy to pick up the slack.

- **Ask other members whether it's an issue for them.** You may be the only one it bothers or the only one on whom she is imposing. If everyone else doesn't mind, then you may choose to grin and bear it. If you are the one on whom she is overrelying, then you need to politely but firmly decline the next time she asks a favor.

- **Talk it over.** If you are tired of one parent not assuming responsibilities, then ask to speak to her without the children present. Without judgment, express your concerns. The individual may not even realize that her behavior is a problem. She may have a valid excuse, but in any case, problem solve together to find a solution that works for all parties.

Sometimes, it's just a clash of personalities. You may not enjoy the company of another member or they are offensive in some way. Your choices are ignore the parent, confront the parent, or if necessary, leave the group (I'll discuss this last option at the end of the chapter).

When a Parent Has a Problem

One of the benefits of joining a play group is the adult friendships. If you are lucky, you develop relationships that last even when the kids have outgrown play group. You may find that one of the adults in the group has a problem or is in the midst of a family crisis. Here's what to do.

If you suspect that a parent has issues that are potentially affecting the children in her care (for example, a problem with substance or alcohol abuse), you may have to intervene. Ask the other parents in the group whether they are worried. If there is a consensus that something is seriously wrong, quietly but carefully present your concerns to the parent. It may be unpleasant, and it's unlikely that there will be an instant resolution to the problem. But if the children are potentially at risk, you may have no choice but to ask her to leave the group. Offer support and friendship, but your first responsibility is for the children's safety.

If a family is in crisis, play group can help. Offer to take the children for play dates. Arrange to bring food to the home. Be ready to listen, sympathize, and support. Be a friend.

ABC **Play Group Chatter**

> I have such memories of the times and conversations at play group. We often talked about television shows, and I'll never forget this one mom in our group talking about an episode where a young mother is diagnosed with breast cancer. We all cried and commiserated about the fictional mom, but it wasn't long after when this same woman in our group was diagnosed with breast cancer. I can still remember what we were wearing when we sat in my playroom and had that conversation.
>
> —Barbara, mother of three

Problem with Someone Else's Child

Sometimes you see a child in the group with an issue that the parent doesn't seem to recognize. Perhaps you have more experience with children and think that the youngster's behavior, motor, or language skills are outside the parameters of what is normal. It's always a touchy subject to comment on someone else's child, but with sensitivity, you should speak up.

If it's a health or developmental issue, early intervention can often help. Suggest that the parent talk to her doctor about the concern. Although the delay may well be within the range of what is considered normal, it's better to be proactive on behalf of a child.

Play Group Don'ts

If you suspect that a child may have a problem, speak to the parent, but don't offer diagnoses. Present what you see, and if you have a recommendation for a professional, offer that name as well.

Child Abuse and Domestic Violence

If you suspect that there are more serious problems in the family, with either a child or an adult, how and when you intervene is important.

If you suspect child neglect, maltreatment, or abuse (physical, emotional, or sexual), you *must* take action. This is not easy, and if you are wrong, it can create a permanent rift between you and the individual. But the alternative—not speaking up—is unacceptable.

According to the Child Abuse Prevention Network, "Don't wait until you can "prove" child abuse— make your report whenever your worries about the safety of a child turn into suspicions that the child is being abused or neglected. Before you call, organize your facts (times, names, places, specific suspicions of abuse or neglect, and other details)." The website www.child-abuse.com/ provides links to child abuse hotlines in every state, or you can call the Childhelp National Child Abuse Hotline, 1-800-4-A-Child.

The Child Welfare Information Gateway (www. childwelfare.gov/pubs/factsheets/signs.cfm) lists the following signs as possibly signaling neglect or abuse.

The child ...

- Shows sudden changes in behavior or school performance.
- Has not received help for physical or medical problems brought to the parents' attention.
- Has learning problems (or difficulty concentrating) that cannot be attributed to specific physical or psychological causes.
- Is always watchful, as though preparing for something bad to happen.
- Lacks adult supervision.
- Is overly compliant, passive, or withdrawn.
- Comes to school or other activities early, stays late, and does not want to go home.

The parent ...

- Shows little concern for the child.
- Denies the existence of—or blames the child for—the child's problems in school or at home.
- Asks teachers or other caretakers to use harsh physical discipline if the child misbehaves.
- Sees the child as entirely bad, worthless, or burdensome.

- Demands a level of physical or academic performance the child cannot achieve.
- Looks primarily to the child for care, attention, and satisfaction of emotional needs.

The parent and child ...

- Rarely touch or look at each other.
- Consider their relationship entirely negative.
- State that they do not like each other.

Types of Abuse

The following signs from the Child Welfare Information Gateway are often associated with particular types of child abuse and neglect. It's important to note, however, that physical abuse, neglect, sexual abuse, and emotional abuse are more typically found in combination than alone. A physically abused child, for example, is often emotionally abused as well, and a sexually abused child also may be neglected.

Signs of Physical Abuse

Consider the possibility of physical abuse if the child:

- Has unexplained burns, bites, bruises, broken bones, or black eyes.
- Has fading bruises or other marks noticeable after an absence from school.

- Seems frightened of the parents and protests or cries when it's time to go home.
- Shrinks at the approach of adults.
- Reports injury by a parent or another adult caregiver.

Consider the possibility of physical abuse if the parent or other adult caregiver:

- Offers conflicting, unconvincing, or no explanation for the child's injury.
- Describes the child as "evil" or in some other very negative way.
- Uses harsh physical discipline with the child.
- Has a history of abuse as a child.

Signs of Neglect

Consider the possibility of neglect if the child:

- Is frequently absent from school.
- Begs for or steals food or money.
- Lacks needed medical or dental care, immunizations, or glasses.
- Is consistently dirty and has severe body odor.
- Lacks sufficient clothing for the weather.
- Abuses alcohol or other drugs.
- States that there is no one at home to provide care.

Consider the possibility of neglect if the parent or other adult caregiver:

- Appears to be indifferent to the child.
- Seems apathetic or depressed.
- Behaves irrationally or in a bizarre manner.
- Is abusing alcohol or other drugs.

Signs of Sexual Abuse

Consider the possibility of sexual abuse if the child:

- Has difficulty walking or sitting.
- Suddenly refuses to change for gym or to participate in physical activities.
- Reports nightmares or bed wetting.
- Experiences a sudden change in appetite.
- Demonstrates bizarre, sophisticated, or unusual sexual knowledge or behavior.
- Becomes pregnant or contracts a venereal disease, particularly if younger than age 14.
- Runs away.
- Reports sexual abuse by a parent or another adult caregiver.

Consider the possibility of sexual abuse if the parent or other adult caregiver:

- Is unduly protective of the child or severely limits the child's contact with other children, especially of the opposite sex.

- Is secretive and isolated.
- Is jealous or controlling with family members.

Signs of Emotional Maltreatment

Consider the possibility of emotional maltreatment if the child:

- Shows extremes in behavior, such as overly compliant or demanding behavior, extreme passivity, or aggression.
- Is either inappropriately adult (parenting other children, for example) or inappropriately infantile (frequently rocking or head-banging, for example).
- Is delayed in physical or emotional development.
- Has attempted suicide.
- Reports a lack of attachment to the parent.

Consider the possibility of emotional maltreatment if the parent or other adult caregiver:

- Constantly blames, belittles, or berates the child.
- Is unconcerned about the child and refuses to consider offers of help for the child's problems.
- Overtly rejects the child.

ABC Play Group Chatter

According to the National Institute of Mental Health, up to 10 million children are exposed to domestic violence directed at their mothers by partners. This puts the children at increased risk for developing behavioral problems, depression, anxiety, and post-traumatic stress disorder.

Domestic Abuse of a Partner

According to the National Domestic Violence Hotline (www.ndvh.org, 1-800-799-7233), domestic violence can be defined as a pattern of behavior in any relationship that is used to gain or maintain power and control over an intimate partner.

Abuse is physical, sexual, emotional, economic, or psychological actions or threats of actions that influence another person. This includes any behaviors that frighten, intimidate, terrorize, manipulate, hurt, humiliate, blame, injure, or wound someone.

Domestic violence can happen to anyone of any race, age, sexual orientation, religion, or gender. It can happen to couples who are married, living together, or who are dating. Domestic violence affects people of all socioeconomic backgrounds and education levels.

If you think you may be in an emotionally, physically, or sexually abusive relationship, take the quiz that the National Domestic Violence Hotline offers on its website www.ndvh.org.

ABC Play Group Chatter

According to the National Women's Health Information Center (www. womenshealth.gov/violence/prevent/ how.cfm), it's important not to place "shame, blame, or guilt" on someone you think is a victim of domestic violence. Rather than insist that she leaves the relationship, it would be more helpful to say something like, "I get scared thinking about what might happen to you."

If you are in such a relationship or suspect that a member of the play group is, here's what the National Domestic Violence Hotline advises:

- Don't be afraid to let that person know that you are concerned for their safety. Help your friend or family member recognize the abuse. Tell him or her that you see what is going on and that you want to help. Help them recognize that what is happening is not normal and that they deserve a healthy, non-violent relationship.

- Acknowledge that he or she is in a very difficult and scary situation. Let your friend or family member know that the abuse is not their fault. Reassure him or her that they are not alone and that there is help and support out there.

- Be supportive. Listen to your friend or family member. Remember that it may be difficult for him or her to talk about the abuse. Let him or her know that you are available to help whenever they may need it. What they need most is someone who will believe and listen to them.

- Be nonjudgmental. Respect your friend or family member's decisions. There are many reasons why victims stay in abusive relationships. He or she may leave and return to the relationship many times. Do not criticize his or her decisions or try to guilt them. He or she will need your support even more during those times.

- Encourage him or her to participate in activities outside of the relationship with friends and family.

- If he or she ends the relationship, continue to be supportive of them. Although the relationship was abusive, your friend or family member may still feel sad and lonely once it's over. He or she will need time to mourn the loss of the relationship and will especially need your support at that time.

- Help him or her to develop a safety plan.

- Encourage him or her to talk to people who can provide help and guidance. Find a local domestic violence agency that provides counseling or support groups. Offer to go with him or her to talk to family and friends. If he or she has to go to the police, court, or a lawyer, offer to go along for moral support.

- Remember that you cannot "rescue" him or her. Although it is difficult to see someone you care about get hurt, ultimately the person getting hurt has to be the one to decide that they want to do something about it. It's important for you to support him or her and help them find a way to safety and peace.

Making a Graceful Exit

You may decide that the play group is not working for your child or for you and that the only solution is to quit. You don't want to burn any bridges should you decide to leave. You will probably see these parents in the community; your child may end up in school with the other children. If at all possible, leave on friendly terms. Here are some suggestions:

- Be sure that the issues that are prompting your decision can't be resolved within the group. Would being honest about your concerns or additional help with your play group responsibilities make a difference in your decision?

- Offer to *try* to find someone to take your place in the play group.

- If there is any financial obligation involved (for example, the group rents space to meet), try to work out a fair settlement if you cannot find a replacement.

The Least You Need to Know

- Don't buy into another parent's competitive behavior.

- Observing conflicting parenting styles in your play group can be an opportunity to see new ways to resolve a problem.

- Be nonjudgmental but candid when you confront a parent who has been slacking in his play group responsibilities.

- If you suspect child abuse, you must report it to the authorities.

- Be supportive if you suspect a parent is a victim of domestic violence, but don't blame, shame, or guilt her.

- If you decide to quit a play group, try to leave on friendly terms.

Celebrating Birthdays, Holidays, and Special Occasions

In This Chapter

- Celebrating birthdays
- Observing holidays
- Welcoming a new sibling

Special occasions, such as birthdays and holidays, are fun to celebrate in play group and present opportunities for children to learn and grow. Parents can decide how they want to handle holidays—especially if the members of the group are of different faiths. Look at it as a chance to teach children about diversity and to embrace differences.

In this chapter, you'll also find strategies for how a play group can help a preschooler adjust to the birth of a new baby in his family. Young children are often excited, confused, and worried when they become a big brother or big sister, and play group can help ease the transition as well as offer respite for tired parents!

Birthday Celebrations

One of the nice things about preschoolers is that birthday celebrations don't need to be elaborate. You may choose to have a separate birthday party for your child, but celebrating at play group may be more than enough.

If you do decide to have a separate party, invite all the children in the play group or none. It's too hard for little ones to avoid chatting about who is on the party list and who isn't. Feelings are easily hurt.

If it's not your turn to host play group when it's your child's birthday, ask to switch days. At a minimum, bring the snack for the day—decorated with candles for the birthday child to blow out. To celebrate the day, why not follow through with a birthday theme in several of the activities?

Play Group Don'ts

Don't devote the entire session to one child's preferences. While it's fine to celebrate a child's special day, it's a play session for all the kids, and their needs must be met, too.

Art Activities

The children can make many birthday-themed art projects. Here are just a few ideas:

- They can construct Play-Doh cakes with clay candles.

- They can construct a birthday banner, with each child decorating a section of the banner. The adults can write "Happy Birthday" and the child's name across the top.
- The children can make cards for the birthday child.
- The children can decorate party hats. Either buy ready-made hats and have the children add glitter, pom-poms, scraps of paper, and so on, or roll a piece of construction paper into a cone, tape it closed, and have the children decorate.

Snack Time

For a birthday snack, bring unfrosted cupcakes, white icing, food coloring, and candy sprinkles to play group. Let each child add a drop or two of the food coloring of his choice to a small bowl of frosting. He can then ice his cupcake and add sprinkles (or other toppings).

Books

Let the birthday child pick the book(s) that will be read to the group. You may also want to choose some books with birthday themes, such as *Clifford's Birthday Party* by Norman Bridwell, *Biscuit's Birthday* by Alyssa Satin Capucilli and Pat Schories, *Arthur's Birthday* by Marc Brown, and *Happy Birthday to You* by Dr. Seuss.

Celebrating Holidays

Whatever the season, religious and secular holidays
are opportunities for children to learn through play.
Art projects and cooking are perfect opportunities
for the youngsters to explore new customs.

You have to decide how comfortable you are per-
mitting your preschooler to participate in another
faith's customs and traditions. If you believe that
the play group is not showing enough sensitivity
to your concerns, speak up. Using language that
applies to all the children can be helpful. For example, it can be as simple as saying you would prefer
that the children make *holiday* gifts, not Christmas
gifts.

You want to teach your children tolerance and
acceptance of our nation's differences while respect-
ing their own heritage. In public schools, according to the Anti-Defamation League (www.adl.
org/issue_education/guide_parents/print.asp), "The
basic guideline you need to remember is that the
public schools can teach about religion as long as
they do not preach religion. Adults—whether they
are teachers, administrators, community leaders,
or parents—must be careful to distinguish between
teaching about a religious holiday and actually celebrating that holiday."

While it's valuable for children to learn about different faiths, it's also important that they learn that
families may celebrate the same holiday in different
ways. It's another chance to reinforce the concept,

"This is how *we* do it in our home." You respect other families' choices but also reinforce your own traditions.

Be ready to share your family's customs and traditions. Not only is it an opportunity for the group members, both adults and kids, to learn something new, but it also gives your child an opportunity to feel proud of his family's heritage. For example, you can have the children make guacamole or enchiladas for a Cinco de Mayo celebration. It's fun for the kids, a nutritious snack, and gives your youngster a chance to shine.

Play Group Do's

If your family blends heritages, you may want to share them all with the group. It validates your child's identity. For example, in an article in *Lilith* magazine, Rabbi Judy Spicehandler explains that for her own Chinese adopted daughter, "I did everything—Chinese, Hebrew, English. I tried to merge the Chinese theme."

Projects to Celebrate the Holiday Season

The commercial hype for the holiday season starts early. All too often, Halloween decorations are barely out of store windows when Christmas decorations go up. But young children don't have an accurate sense of time. They don't understand that the holiday is months away. Whatever celebration activities your group chooses to do, keep it close to the actual date of the holiday.

Here are some ideas for how the play group might celebrate the holiday season.

Picture Frame

Materials needed for each frame:

> Photo of each child or group photo
>
> Ready-made photo frame or ready-made cardboard matting (available from craft stores)
>
> Colored markers
>
> Glitter, feathers, stones, rubber stamps, and ink to decorate the frames
>
> Glue as necessary
>
> Optional: small magnets, tissue paper, or kraft paper

Have the youngsters decorate either ready-made frames or cardboard matting using the colored markers, glitter, feathers, stones, and so on.

If desired, use rubber stamps to decorate tissue gift wrap or kraft paper to use to wrap the picture frame. Or, buy small magnets from a local hardware store and glue them to the back of the frame so it can be displayed on the refrigerator.

Menorah

Materials needed for each menorah:

> Wooden blocks, one long and one short per child

Paint and paintbrush

Wood glue

Nine metal nuts

Chanukah candles

Glue the smaller block in the middle of the larger block. Paint the wood blocks. After the paint dries, glue eight nuts on the larger block, spreading them out evenly. Glue one nut on the smaller block. Insert candles into the nuts.

Charity Projects for Preschoolers

Although you can opt to exchange gifts among the play group, another idea is to encourage the children to make gifts for others. The gifts can be for their families but also can be a charity project that the group does together. Here are some age-appropriate ideas that tap into interests that preschoolers can understand:

- Have the children collect dog and cat food, treats, and toys to donate to the local animal shelter. You can extend the concept by reading books on dogs or cats as well as making a group card to give to the shelter with the donation.

- Have each family go through their child's clothes and bring in those they've outgrown. Have the children help box up the clothes, with a card from the children, to donate to a shelter. You can extend the collection to children's books and toys, but make sure that the child is comfortable donating the item.

- Have a play group penny jar. Each session, have the children contribute pennies and then donate the money to a child-focused charity. Besides teaching about charities, counting the pennies is a good premath skill.

- Have the children bring a nonperishable food item to each play group session to be donated to a local food pantry. They can help decorate a box or bag to store the items.

- Around major holidays, have the play group plan a meal to be donated to a local shelter. Take a group field trip to the local supermarket and purchase the items, or assign specific items for each family to purchase.

Halloween Art Project

This is a fun project that celebrates the season but isn't too scary for young children.

Handprint Spiders

Materials needed:

Black tempera paint

Paper

Googly eyes

Glue

Soap and water to clean up

Paint each child's hand and fingers (not the thumb) with black paint. Have the child press his hand and fingers down on the paper—but not his thumb. Turn the paper around and have him press his hand and fingers down on the paper, right next to the original impression. Glue googly eyes in the center, and you have an eight-legged spider!

For added fun, display the spiders. You could have the children paste a magnet on the back and each can take home his project to display on the refrigerator. Another idea? The adults could cut out the spiders, put a piece of string through the top, and hang them for a seasonal display.

When you're done, wash up thoroughly with soap and water.

May Day Projects

May Day, celebrated on May 1, marks the beginning of spring (although the first day of spring is officially March 20). Here are some ideas for helping the children enjoy the new season:

- Have each child plant marigold seeds in a small paper cup or pot. Discuss plant care with the children, including giving the plant plenty of water and sun.

- Create a May Pole by hanging ribbons (one for each child) from a clothesline. Turn on some music and let the children, each holding on to a ribbon, weave in and out to create an intricate pattern.

- Have the children create May baskets, filled with flowers and small treats. Traditionally, you surprised a friend by leaving the basket on his or her doorstep, ringing the bell, and running away. The play group could practice a variation of this tradition: surprise the parents with the baskets at the end of the session.

Fourth of July Project

This Independence Day project can be done so that each child creates a small flag, or they can work together to make a large one. It's an opportunity to practice math skills by counting the number of stars needed as well as the number of red stripes (seven) needed for each flag.

Grand Old Flag

Materials needed:

> White paper
>
> Blue and red construction paper
>
> Child-safe scissors
>
> Glue or paste
>
> White glue-on or stick-on stars, or white tempera paint
>
> Popsicle sticks

For each flag, have the children cut out seven red strips and one blue square. If children don't have the facility to use scissors yet, the adults can prepare the strips ahead of time.

On the white paper, paste down the red strips, starting at the top with a red stripe and ending at the bottom with a red stripe. The white stripes of the flag are created by the white of the paper showing between the red stripes.

In the left-hand corner of the paper, glue down a blue rectangle.

A child can paste down 50 stars. There are five rows of six stars each (beginning with the top row), alternating with four rows of five stars each. Alternatively, a child can dip his thumb in white tempera paint and make thumbprints to represent stars. If you are making one very large flag as a group project, the children can make handprints for the stars.

For individual flags, staple the paper to a popsicle stick.

Play Group Welcomes a New Baby

Preschoolers often view the arrival of a new baby in their family with a mixture of excitement and a great deal of concern. Common worries are a fear of being displaced by the new sibling, a fear of sharing parents and their home (toys, space, grandparents, and so on), and a general fear of change. Behavior regression is a frequent result. The toilet-trained child may suddenly have "accidents"; the child who has been drinking from a cup may suddenly insist on having a bottle. If your group allows for some parents to leave during the session, then the youngster may suffer separation anxiety where none had existed prebaby. (See Chapter 3 for tips on handling separation anxiety.)

> ### ABC Play Group Chatter
>
> When her little sister was born, my older daughter's play group was our key to life! The planned event gave us structure and something to look forward to each week during a time when so much was unpredictable with a newborn!
>
> —Kate, mother of three

Play group can serve as a stabilizing force for a new big brother/big sister. If you have been meeting regularly, keeping to the schedule reassures a young child that his life will not totally change with a new baby on the scene. Seeing how other children his age deal with siblings gives him role models for his own behavior. If you can't bring your child to play group, make arrangements with another parent (with whom he is comfortable) or family member (such as a grandparent) to take him.

Some play group activities to welcome a new baby include the following:

- Have the children in the play group make individual welcome cards for the baby and a banner for the older child's room that says, "I'm a Big Brother (Sister)."

- Read books to the group about a new baby in the family. Some good ones for this age group include *Hi New Baby* by Robie H. Harris, *Will There Be a Lap for Me* by Dorothy Corey, and *I Used to Be the Baby* by Robin Ballard.

- Have the older child bring a special snack to play group to celebrate becoming a big brother or sister.

- Have plenty of dolls and stuffed animals on hand at play group so the older sibling and the other children can role play taking care of their babies.

The Least You Need to Know

- Celebrating a birthday at play group can be just the right level of excitement for young children.

- Celebrate holidays with sensitivity to the customs and traditions of all play group families.

- Play group can be a stabilizing force for a youngster who has just become a big brother or big sister.

Easy and Fun Indoor Activities

In This Chapter

- Art projects: it's the process, not the product
- Making merry with music
- Stretching the imagination with dramatic play
- Simple science projects
- Cooking up fun in the kitchen

Children like structure. That doesn't mean that you need to plan every minute of the play group session, but having one or more planned activities for the children is fun, builds camaraderie, and has educational value as well.

In this chapter, you'll find indoor activities for your play group. Because children develop at different rates, you may need to adapt or modify an activity to your child's abilities.

Art Projects for the Young

Always remember when doing art projects with children that it's the process, not the product, which is important. You want to give children the opportunity to express themselves in various media. "Picture-perfect pictures" suggest too much parental involvement in the art projects. The refrigerator gallery of your child's art may well be a jumble of scribbles and unformed shapes, and that's fine. Art stimulates your child's creative side while he also learns about color and spatial dimensions. He gains fine motor control as he experiments with crayons, tempera and finger paints, watercolors, clay, cutting, and pasting.

Homemade Play Dough

You can certainly buy Play-Doh or other soft modeling clays, but making your own is exciting for kids. Playing with clay is an excellent way to improve fine motor control (it can strengthen hand and finger muscles). Children can make free-form sculptures but also enjoy using cookie cutters to make shapes and forms to mold three-dimensional objects. They can practice cutting the dough using child-sized scissors (which also strengthens hand muscles).

ABC **Play Group Chatter**

To create art, children must organize, reason, invent, and solve problems.

—Don Bower, extension human development specialist, University of Georgia and Fort Valley State University

An adult must carefully supervise the cooking phase of this project. You can use food coloring, packets of Kool-Aid, or packets of Jell-O to color the dough. The children can measure and add the ingredients. The adult then needs to stir it over the stove. Children can knead the dough once it's ready. Stored in an airtight container, the dough will not dry out and can be reused repeatedly.

Materials needed:

1 cup flour

$^1/_2$ cup salt

1 cup water

1 TB. vegetable oil

1 $^1/_2$ tsp. cream of tartar

Coloring

Mix all ingredients in a saucepan over low heat. To avoid scorching the bottom of the mixture, stir constantly for about three to five minutes. Dough is ready when it rolls into a ball. Cool dough for 15 to 30 minutes before handing it to children for kneading.

Bug Days

To expand the value of these art projects, make bugs the theme of the day!

- Have the children compare their crafted "bugs" with those found in nature.

- They can make their own versions as fanciful as they want, but through pictures or actual specimens (but be sure to catch and release), talk about those found in nature. Ask why bugs have antennae; ask about the number of legs an insect has compared to humans and other animals; and question them about the difference between a bug and a spider.

- Make "bugs on a log" for a snack (have children fill celery stalks with peanut butter or cream cheese, and top them with raisin "bugs").

Children can fashion bugs from the homemade play dough they made or can make bugs from one of these projects.

Materials needed:

Empty egg crates

Paint, markers, and crayons

Pipe cleaners

Googly or pom-pom eyes

Glue

Before the play group arrives, cut the egg crates in half lengthwise and poke three parallel holes on each side for the legs. Make two holes on one end for the antennae. The bugs are fashioned by turning the crates upside down and decorating them.

Play Group Do's

While a preschooler's art smock can be a father's old shirt, consider investing in a plastic or vinyl smock for easier cleanup and no bleed-through of paint. Art smocks protect your child's clothes from paint, glue, and other materials. Each child should bring an art smock to all play group sessions.

Give each child half of a crate and at least three or four cups. The child can then paint or color the cups. He can thread pipe cleaners through parallel holes to fashion legs (a caterpillar has six legs—three on each side). Alternatively, he can omit the legs and just use pipe cleaners for antennae. Last, have the child draw on the mouth and glue on the eyes.

A single cup of the egg crate can also be used to make a ladybug or spider (make four holes on each side to fashion eight legs).

Play Group Don'ts

Don't assume that you know what a child has created. Ask him to explain his "bug" to you.

Let's Make Music

According to KidsHealth.org, "Research has shown that children who are actively involved in music (who play it or sing it regularly) do better in reading and math when they start school, are better able to focus and control their bodies, play better with others, and have higher self-esteem."

Have the children make musical instruments. You can decide whether you want everyone to make the same instrument or offer a choice. Once they've created their instruments, you can extend the activity in several ways:

- Have the kids choose a name for their band.
- Put on some music and have them accompany it with their instruments.
- Have the kids create their own music with the instruments or accompany their own singing with their instruments.
- Put together a marching band. To add to the excitement, have the kids create "band hats" by gluing tall feathers to baseball caps.
- Record the band and make a CD or tape for each child.

Tambourine

Materials needed:

> Heavy-duty paper plates
>
> Stapler
>
> Masking or scotch tape
>
> Hole punch
>
> Markers or crayons
>
> Decorative items such as feathers, decals, stickers, or glitter to glue on (optional)
>
> Small jingle bells (available in craft stores)
>
> String or yarn

Before the children arrive, an adult should staple the plates together (two plates facing each other) and cover each staple with tape. Punch six holes evenly spaced around the plate.

The children can then decorate the plates with markers or crayons and other items. Have them tie individual jingle bells to plates with the string or yarn (they may need the assistance of an adult). Shake to play.

Drum

Materials needed for each child:

> Empty oatmeal canister with lid
>
> Construction paper

Glue

Crayons or markers

Two unsharpened pencils

Before the children arrive, cut construction paper to the size of the oatmeal canister.

Children can use the markers or crayons to decorate the construction paper and then glue the construction paper around the canister. Use unsharpened pencils as drumsticks, or have the children use their hands to beat the drum (like a bongo drum).

Horn

Materials needed for each child:

Paper towel roll

Waxed paper

Rubber band

Before the children arrive, poke several holes in the paper towel roll.

Children can then cover one end of the roll with a piece of waxed paper, securing the waxed paper to the roll with a rubber band. Play by humming or singing into the open end of the horn. Have children experiment by covering one or more of the holes in the shaft.

Cymbals

These are noisy but fun. Let each child have a turn playing the cymbals. All you need are two pot lids with knobs for handles. Play by striking the two lids together.

Dramatic Play

Dramatic play develops a child's language skills as well as encourages his creativity. Videotape the children's dramatic play so that they can watch movies of themselves. Children will develop more sophisticated dramatic play, making up stories and role-playing, as they grow older.

ABC Play Group Chatter

I had a good laugh when I overheard the kids playing doctor's office during play group, one of their favorite pretend scenarios. My daughter always wanted to be the receptionist and she engaged in this long, one-sided conversation with a patient. All I could hear her say was "So, you're smoking? No, we don't have ..." and then she named a particular brand of nicotine patch, "... at this office." I thought it was hysterical that she obviously watched a lot of television, but had also learned, and was passing on, the dangers of smoking.

—Maggie, mother of two

Favorite Tales from a Different Point of View

This game helps children see that there are two (or more) sides to every story.

- Have the children tell a favorite fairy tale; for example, *The Three Little Pigs.*
- Now have the children act out the story, assigning each child a role. The children will make up their own dialogue to tell the story.
- It's time to switch things up. Now have the children tell the same story but from another point of view. For example, the original story is from the pigs' point of view. But have the children tell the story as the Big Bad Wolf saw it. Maybe the Big Bad Wolf isn't so bad. Maybe he just wanted to play with the pigs. Maybe he wasn't huffing and puffing to blow the house down but was just sneezing a lot! Let the children's imagination wander, and come up with different scenarios for these tales.

Puppet Theater

You can have the children create their own puppets (decorated paper plates with a popsicle stick to hold the puppet) or use store-bought puppets. (Lost a sock in the wash? Save single socks to use for puppets. Children can glue on yarn for hair, googly eyes, and a piece of felt for a mouth.) The puppet show can be the theme of the day's play group session, beginning with an art project to make the puppets as well as tickets or invitations for the audience (parents). They can also make post-show refreshments.

You can make this project simple or more complex depending on the age and interest of the children. Videotape the show so the children can see it once it's over.

The stage can be an empty appliance box with an opening cut out of the bottom. The children kneel down and hold the puppets up for the audience to see.

You can use a familiar fairy tale or have the children create their own story (practice with them so they know what happens next).

Science Projects

Exploring the world helps preschoolers learn to distinguish between reality and fantasy. Science projects also provide the opportunity for young children to develop their premath skills as they learn to measure, compare, and contrast. They are also developing language skills as they discuss the results of their science projects.

Play Group Do's

A great resource for science, math, and reading activities for young children can be found at www.pbs.org/parents/childdevelopment/.

Plants, Trees ... and Celery?

This project teaches children how water rises up the veins in the stalks of plants and trees.

Materials needed for each child:

Clear plastic cup (print the name of the child on his or her cup)

Water

Food dye

Stalk of celery with the end freshly cut

Fill each cup halfway with water. Have each child choose a color of food dye, and mix a few drops into the water. Set the stalk of celery upright in the water. The children will take the cup home with them.

After a few days, the child will discover that the "strings" of the celery are the same color as the water. Parents should then cut the stalk crosswise so that the children can examine the colored areas (the veins of the celery).

Measure Up

This is an easy, fun way to help a child learn the concept of bigger than/smaller than.

Materials needed for each child:

> Masking tape
>
> Ruler or tape measure
>
> Pencil
>
> Construction paper

On a table, place a group of objects of varying sizes—such as books, stuffed animals, mugs, combs, brushes, barrettes, and spoons—and create multiple labels for each object from masking tape.

Give each child a ruler and a pencil. Show them how to measure an object from top to bottom. With a pencil, the child should make a mark on the ruler to record the object's height. He should take the label for the object and place it on a piece of construction paper. Under the label, the child will draw a line from the bottom of the ruler to the mark he has made for the object's height.

When everyone has finished measuring five objects, the group can discuss which is the biggest and smallest. If you have a postal or food scale, you can also help the children discover the heaviest and lightest objects.

Cooking

Children learn about nutrition as well as important mathematical concepts when they help cook. They also may be tempted to try new foods when in the company of other more adventurous eaters. Remind children that they must wash their hands with soap and water before handling food.

Pudding Paint

This fun project is messy for sure, but cleanup is easy because the ingredients are also edible! Be sure each child has a smock to wear.

Materials needed:

> Instant vanilla pudding (you can use sugar-free or fat-free varieties if desired)
>
> Milk for preparing pudding
>
> Muffin tins or cups
>
> Food coloring
>
> Plain paper or parchment paper

Follow the package directions for making instant pudding. The children can help measure the milk and pour it into the bowl. Each child can take a turn mixing the pudding with a spoon.

Ladle the pudding into muffin tins or cups. The children can choose which food colors they want to incorporate into the pudding. (You can discuss what color is created when you mix two different colors; for example, red and yellow create orange.)

The children can then finger paint on the paper
with the pudding.

Play Group Do's

Put measuring cups in the sandbox or
in the bath. Your child will discover
simple math concepts. For example, it
takes two half-cups of sand to fill the one-
cup measure.

Pizza Party

For a snack, have the children create their own pizzas.

Materials needed:

Individual-sized plain pizza crusts (one for each
child), or buy pizza dough from a local pizzeria
and have the children knead and roll out the
dough

Toppings: peppers, cheese, olives, pineapple
slices, tomatoes, mushrooms, pepperoni, sau-
sage

Let the children design their own pizzas. Have
them make a face out of the vegetables. Adults will
bake the pizzas.

Extend the cooking project by cutting out pictures
of foods. Mark different pages with the food groups
important to health: grains (breads, pasta, and rice);
vegetables; fruits; dairy (milk, ice cream, yogurt,

and cheese); and proteins (meat, poultry, fish, and legumes). Have the children paste their favorites of each category on the page. Bind the books with staples (cover the staples with tape), and have each child decorate the cover.

The Least You Need to Know

- With any activity, it's the process more than the product that is important.

- Art projects allow children to express themselves in various media and improve their fine motor control.

- Making music is fun and also reinforces prereading skills as children learn about rhythm and beats.

- Dramatic play lets children experience life from a different perspective.

- Science projects offer young children the opportunity to explore their world, as well as reinforce math and language skills.

- Cooking with children is an opportunity to teach nutrition as well as encourage them to try new foods.

Outdoor Play Activities

In This Chapter

- Fun and educational field trips
- Safety precautions
- Activities for the playground or backyard
- Exploring nature

Just going outside, regardless of what activities the children do, always changes the dynamic. Squabbling toddlers calm down when they walk out of the house—even if it's just to walk down the driveway to pick up the mail.

According to the National Association for the Education of Young Children, "Our society has become increasingly complex, but there remains a need for every child to feel the sun and wind on his cheek and engage in self-paced play. Children's attempts to make their way across monkey bars, negotiate the hopscotch course, play jacks, or toss a football require intricate behaviors of planning, balance, and strength—traits we want to encourage in children."

Preschoolers have boundless amounts of energy. Going outside is a perfect outlet. They'll enjoy and benefit from the freedom to run, climb, mosey, explore, and touch and smell nature. But it's crucial to establish clear safety rules for any outside excursion. In this chapter, you'll find the information you need to take fun, safe field trips and to play safely outdoors as well as tips on how to explore nature with young children.

Field Trips for Preschoolers

Traveling with children, near or far, always seems like it requires the same amount of planning as moving an army battalion. Don't let the pesky details stop you from taking a trip with your group. Field trips have several benefits:

- They are educational and fun.
- They provide a break in the routine.
- They offer kids an opportunity to collect information from the source rather than from a book (it's one thing to read about a fire engine, but how much more exciting is it to visit the fire station and climb on one?).
- They afford children the chance to develop their language and social skills.

Especially for young children, traveling is tiring (and for the accompanying adults, too!). Go when the children are rested, and limit the amount of time traveling and exploring the new locale. It's better to go back for another visit than to experience a group of preschoolers having meltdowns from exhaustion.

Play Group Do's

Before going on a field trip, get a permission slip for each child. It's probably unnecessary but legally prudent.

Field trips don't have to involve much travel. A walking field trip, even if it's just around the block, can provide children with a chance to explore nature. Instead of driving, walk to the fire station, library, or playground. It's good exercise for kids and parents! (See "Traveling by Foot" later in the chapter for some safety precautions.) Here are some ideas:

- Walk around the neighborhood to explore the leaves that different kinds of trees produce. Here is a link to a photo of tree leaves to help with identification: www. discoverscience.rutgers.edu/extras/trees/treephotos.html. Point out the difference between deciduous trees (which lose their leaves in the fall) and evergreens (which keep their foliage year-round).

  To extend the educational value of this trip, pick up some twigs or leaves for the children to use for collages. Or, help the children make a map of the neighborhood, marking off streets and houses.

- Check out neighborhood signs ("No Parking," street names, stop signs, yield signs, speed limit signs, and historical markers). You can discuss the meaning of the signs but also the colors, shapes, and number of sides on the signs.

  To extend the educational value of this trip, have the children make some road signs: address signs for their own homes or signs for their own rooms. They can also make stop signs or pictures of red and green lights, then play a game of Stop (hold up the red light and everyone has to stop moving) and Go (hold up the green light and everyone moves around until they see the red light flashed).

- Check out a new house or building that is going up in the neighborhood. Revisit the site as the building progresses.

  To extend the educational value of this trip, take pictures of each stage of construction and make a poster with the children. Look for books on construction. Have the children use blocks to build their own houses.

- Explore the clouds. On a warm, partly cloudy day, take blankets outside and have the children lay down on their backs. Have the children describe the shapes that they see, but also point out the different kinds of clouds. Here is a link to a cloud atlas: www.clouds-online.com.

To extend the educational value of this trip, follow up with a simple cotton ball art project, in which each child glues cotton balls on paper to create his or her own cloud panorama. For a more complex discussion of clouds and weather, here are directions for creating a tornado in a bottle: www.wikihow. com/Make-a-Tornado-in-a-Bottle.

Some other field trips may not be within walking distance:

- Take the bus (or commuter train) one stop. Many kids have been on airplanes but have never ridden on local public transportation. Take the children for a ride on the bus or local train. You can go just one stop, have a snack (bring it with you), and take the bus (train) back home. Read books before and after the trip, and have the kids compare their experiences with what they have read.

  To extend the educational value of this trip, make your own train using chairs or boxes. Sing songs about buses ("The Wheels on the Bus") and trains ("I've Been Working on the Railroad").

- Explore a local farmers' market or a neighbor's vegetable garden (be sure to ask for permission first). One little boy didn't realize that French fries are made from potatoes. Talk about the vegetables they see, the colors of the veggies, and the different produce available in different seasons.

To extend the educational value of this trip, plant seeds in a paper cup for the children to take home and watch grow. Talk about produce grown locally and that which is imported (for example, bananas). For a snack, try some new vegetables or fruits.

Safety First

Whether you are just going into the backyard, taking a stroll around the neighborhood, or traveling to some more distant locales, you need to be ready to deal with emergencies.

You should have a minimum of one adult for every two children (and more is better). Ideally, a parent or caregiver will accompany every child if going any distance, especially with younger children.

For any field trip, one of the adults should carry a backpack with the following items:

- Cell phone
- First-aid kit
- Wet wipes or hand sanitizer
- Tissues
- Several gallon-sized zipper bags for trash disposal
- Emergency contact list for all children

If the children are still in diapers, the accompanying adult should carry a backpack that includes a change of clothes, diaper wipes, and clean diapers.

Traveling by Car

When transporting members of the play group by car, here are important safety rules to follow:

- Every child should be in a car safety seat.
- Never permit a child to sit on an adult's lap when riding in the car.
- Never permit a child to use an adult seatbelt instead of a car safety seat.
- Never place a child in a rear-facing car safety seat in the front seat of the vehicle if the car has passenger airbags.
- All children younger than 13 are safer when riding in the back seat.
- Make sure that all hands, fingers, feet, and toes are in the car before you close the car door.
- Never leave children alone in the car.
- On hot days, cover car safety seats with towels and place windshield shades on both the front and back windows to reduce the temperature inside the car.

Check the American Academy of Pediatrics website for more tips on car safety seats: www.aap.org/family/carseatguide.htm.

Traveling by Foot

Going anywhere with a bunch of children is like herding cats. Even with the best of intentions, you need to be super vigilant when walking with kids. They should be holding hands, either with another child or with an adult.

When you're walking down a sidewalk with a group of preschoolers, at a minimum there should be an adult at the front of the line and one at the back of the line. It's even better if there is an adult to hold every child's hand (that is, an adult can escort two children, one on each hand). Some daycare facilities have the children hold onto a rope, held at either end by adults, so that the kids walk safely in the line. If there are no sidewalks, have the children keep as far over on the shoulder of the road as possible and walk facing traffic.

Playground/Backyard Activities

Outdoor play is always a good, healthy diversion. Children will have the opportunity for exercise, dramatic play, and nature exploration. They learn about taking turns on the equipment as well as sharing the toys.

Play Group Don'ts

Don't let a gentle rain or snow on the ground stop you from scheduling some outdoor playtime. (Don't go outside if there is thunder and/or lightning, however.) Dress the children appropriately, and then venture outside. Don't forget to apply sunscreen—even on cloudy days.

Playground Safety

In Chapter 4, I reviewed safety issues for playground equipment. It's also important to make sure that children learn how to play on the equipment. Make sure that all the children understand the rules of playground safety and use playground equipment properly.

Swings safety:

- The child should sit, not stand, on the swings and hold on with both hands.
- Only one child per swing seat.
- Teach children not to walk or run in front of or in back of swings.

Slide safety:

- Climb up the ladder of the slide rather than up the slide itself.
- Slide down feet first and sitting up.

- Don't start down the slide without checking the bottom of the slide to be sure that earlier sliders have moved away from the equipment.

- Remind children not to push or shove, even if they get impatient that the youngster in front of them is slow to move.

- Don't slide down in groups.

Jungle gym/climbing equipment safety:

- Make sure the area is clear of other children before jumping off a piece of equipment.

- Climb down carefully and look out for those who are climbing up.

- Permit children to climb only on age-appropriate/size-appropriate equipment.

- Teach children, when climbing off equipment, to bend their knees and land on both feet.

Play Group Don'ts

Don't let your child wear clothing with drawstrings, carry purses with long straps, or wear necklaces when on playground equipment. The strings can get snagged on the equipment and possibly strangle a child.

Seesaw safety:

- Children sharing a seesaw should be of equal weight, rather than doubling up on one side. And the same rule for swings applies here, too: one child per seat.

- Children should face one another, not ride backward.

- Teach children to hold on with both hands and never to use their hands to push off the ground. They should keep their feet out to the sides rather than underneath the seesaw.

Play Group Don'ts

The Consumer Product Safety Commission advises that children younger than six should not use a full-size trampoline. They urge close supervision for children on trampolines. For more information, go to www.cpsc.gov/CPSCPUB/PUBS/085.html.

Other Outdoor Activities

While the children can play on the equipment, dig in a sandbox, and even run under the sprinklers, here are some fun, easy outdoor activities for your play group:

- **Car Wash.** Have the children wash their riding equipment. Have sponges for each child and several shallow bowls of soapy water. This is best when done in swimsuits because a change of clothes will probably be needed. As with all water activities, close adult supervision is a must.

- **Chalk Talk.** Give each child a piece of jumbo-sized chalk (easier for young hands to manipulate). Have them draw on the sidewalk or driveway.

- **Mural Time.** Use clothes pins to attach a large piece of plastic cloth or kraft paper to string hung between two trees or to a fence. Let the children paint a mural with tempera paints.

- **Hula Hoops.** Kids can try to spin them around their middles. You can also lay the hoops on the ground and have children practice following directions (a skill in itself) by setting up a race course, hopping in and out of the hoops, skipping some hoops—whatever is fun.

- **Treasure Hunt.** Hide some toys in the backyard and give the children picture puzzle clues to find them. For example, you could hide a toy under one of the trees in the backyard and give them a picture of a tree as one of the clues.

- **Camp Out.** If you have a small tent, put it up. Otherwise, use blankets and sheets strung over lawn chairs to create a faux tent. Give each child a flashlight. You can put them in a circle to make a pretend campfire. Or, you can have the youngsters collect twigs and make a pretend campfire (do not create a real fire). Eat snacks in the tent. You can also do this activity inside; it's especially fun on a rainy day.

Exploring Nature with Preschoolers

Preschoolers' natural curiosity makes exploring nature fun for both kids and adults. You don't need to go to a nature preserve to learn about the environment. The backyard or local playground is just fine. Check out the National Park Service website for an educational series on exploring nature with children: www.nps.gov/webrangers/easy/tour2/rockpark/index.html.

Here are some activities that are fun for young children and adults.

Feed the Birds

Take a nature walk and play a game of "I Spy." See how many different color birds you can find. Listen for bird sounds. See whether you can see any birds' nests. Then, have each child make a bird feeder to take home and hang in their yard or on a balcony.

Simple Cereal Bird Feeder

Materials needed:

Lengths of yarn or string, enough for each child, each piece two feet long

Cellophane tape

Donut-shaped cereal (such as Cheerios)

Straws or popsicle sticks

Before children arrive, put a piece of cellophane tape on the end of a length of yarn. Tie a popsicle stick or straw on the other end.

Have the children thread the yarn through the cereal. When done, remove the stick or straw and tie the ends together. Hang outside.

Alternatively, the children can thread pieces of stale bread onto the yarn. To extend the activity, have the children cut out shapes in the bread with cookie cutters before threading.

Bagel Bird Feeder

Materials needed:

Bagels, sliced in half

Cornmeal

Shortening

Bird seed

Yarn

Before children arrive, mix shortening and cornmeal and put in a shallow pan (pie pan). Put bird seed in a separate shallow pan.

Children can dip the cut side of the bagel in the shortening mixture, then into the bird seed.

Thread yarn through the bagel hole and hang outside.

Pinecone Bird Feeder

Materials needed:

> Large pinecones
>
> Cornmeal
>
> Shortening
>
> Bird seed
>
> Shallow pans
>
> Yarn

Before children arrive, mix cornmeal and shortening and put in a shallow pan (pie pan). Put bird seed in a separate shallow pan.

Children can roll the pinecones in the shortening mix. Have them roll them several times to get the mixture into the crevices. Next, roll the pinecones in the bird seed.

Let the pinecones harden overnight, then tie the yarn through the top of the pinecone and hang outside.

Rock and Roll

Materials needed:

> Small paper bags (one for each child)
>
> Egg crates, paint, glue, and felt (if desired)

Give each child a small paper bag and walk outside to collect rocks. Talk about the size, texture, color, and shapes of the rocks they find. Extend the activity by reading books on how rocks are created, such as *Rocks and Minerals* (DK Publishing, 2004) and *Painting on Rocks for Kids* (North Light Books, 2002). Sort the rocks into piles (classification is an important prereading and premath skill). The children can decide to sort by size, color, or other criteria. Display the rock collection in egg crates. The children can create paperweights by washing a large rock, painting it, and gluing felt on the bottom.

ABC Play Group Chatter

At the beginning of May, my son's play group helped me plant tomato, cucumber, and pepper seedlings. Every time the group met at our house that summer, the kids loved to check on "their" vegetables, water them, and eventually, by the end of the summer, eat them for snack.

—Amy, mother of two

Make a Volcano

Materials needed:

> Sand or dirt
>
> Food coloring
>
> Vinegar
>
> Baking soda

Supervise this project carefully. Do not allow children to taste the liquid.

Have the children form a volcano by shaping the sand or dirt into a large cone-shaped pile. Leave a hole in the top for the materials. Add a few drops of food coloring to $1/2$ cup vinegar. Combine two tablespoons baking soda and colored vinegar, and pour immediately into the hole to watch the volcano "erupt."

Extend the activity by discussing the forces of nature with the children. Read books on volcanoes; for example, *Jump into Science: Volcano!* (National Geographic Children's Books, 2007). For a terrific age-appropriate website, visit Volcano World Kids' Door: http://volcano.und.nodak.edu/vwdocs/kids/kids.html/. It's a Collaborative Higher Education, K-12, and Public Outreach project of the North Dakota and Oregon Space Grant Consortia administered by the Department of Geosciences at Oregon State University.

Nature Up Close

Have the children examine nature closely with magnifying glasses. They'll be able to see details in nature that are easy to miss. Set up specimens on a table outdoors. Have them help you collect pinecones, leaves, pods, rocks, and shells.

Listen for animal sounds and see whether the children can identify what they hear: birds, dogs, cats, bees, and other flying insects.

Books of Nature Rubbings

Extend these outdoor activities by making nature rubbings.

Materials needed:

> Thin paper or waxed paper
>
> Rocks, stones, twigs, leaves, tree bark (can also put paper over fences, tables, chairs, or other outdoor objects)
>
> Crayons with paper wrapper removed

Have the child put a thin piece of paper or waxed paper over a twig, piece of tree bark, stone, and so on. Using the long side of the crayon, rub lightly to create an impression of the object. You can collect the rubbings into individual books for each child or make a large one for all the play group members. Later, at story time, "read" the nature rubbing book and have the children discuss what each rubbing represents.

The Least You Need to Know

- Besides being fun and educational, field trips help build a child's social skills.
- Time field trips so that the children are rested. Keep the trips short enough so that no one gets overtired.
- Close adult supervision is critically important when taking the children outdoors. Take other safety precautions, as well.
- Examining nature up close gives children a better understanding of their world.

Learning While Playing

In This Chapter

- Learning prereading and premath skills through play
- Practicing social skills
- Building self-esteem and a sense of competency
- Outdoor play, free play, and cooperative play
- Don't forget cleanup time!

"Play is the work of the child," advised renowned early childhood educator Maria Montessori (1870–1952). When your youngster builds with blocks, dresses up as a pirate or princess, pretends to cook (or actually does help you cook), climbs the jungle gym, listens and tells stories, paints and pastes art projects—all of this playtime nurtures and encourages a child's physical, emotional, social, and intellectual development. There's a wealth of learning going on during playtime, and you don't need to buy a toy stamped "educational" in order for your little one to benefit. In fact, you could just give your child the box and forget the toy. An empty carton encourages imaginative play as the preschooler transforms the box into a spaceship, treasure chest, or even a costume!

In this chapter, we discuss many play group activities and lessons learned while having fun.

Reading and 'Rithmetic Through Play

Without fanfare and through play, your child is acquiring the skills she'll need to read long before she can actually decode the words on a page. As she helps put a napkin at each place for snack time, she is acquiring premath skills that will eventually help her complete complex mathematical calculations.

Reading and math skills require abstract thinking. It's that intellectual leap that moves a child from seeing just a jumble of symbols on a page to understanding that those are letters—and that letters combine to make words. Similarly, there's a difference between rote recitation of numbers as a child counts to 10 or even 100 and a real comprehension that the numbers she rattles off actually correspond to the concrete number of napkins she is distributing.

Circle Time

When children join you on the floor for storytelling and singing, these "chats" are an opportunity for youngsters to learn how to organize their thoughts. When they tell a make-believe story or recall a real-life event, they learn how to structure a tale with a beginning, middle, and end. When they sing childhood favorites such as "The Itsy Bitsy Spider" or "On Top of Spaghetti," they're learning shared knowledge. That's the information that society assumes you know. For example, if someone compares a sports victory to David beating Goliath, most adults would understand the metaphor. Learning common folk songs is part of a child's "informal" education.

Music Appreciation/Creative Movement

Music is the universal language. Without words, it can express emotions and feelings. Similarly, creative movement taps into a child's artistic side and allows him to communicate without words.

As they listen to music, children learn important prereading skills. They can pound out, on store-bought or homemade drums, the rhythmic patterns of the melody as well as learn about opposites and similarities: fast, slow, loud, soft, one at a time, and all together. They can take this same skill and apply it to words in a story (one beat for each syllable). The imagination knows no limits.

Play Group Do's

Have children create their own stories in response to the music they hear. The classic tale of "Peter and the Wolf" by Sergei Prokofiev assigns a different instrument and musical theme for each animal.

Creative movement is an artistic way to promote physical fitness. It also helps children gain control of their bodies. They can move to the rhythm of music (again, a prereading skill) or use their imaginations to simulate something (a falling leaf, for example).

Art Projects

The best art projects are open-ended. They let a child learn that his creativity is limited only by his imagination. Transforming everyday objects, such as empty paper towel rolls and egg cartons, into sculptures, bugs, and alien creatures broadens a child's vision of the world.

Art projects also develop a child's fine motor skills. Drawing with a magic marker and cutting with scissors requires small muscle control. These same fine motor skills will be used to button coats, print letters, and cut with a knife.

Building with Blocks

Playing with blocks is often a favorite activity—
especially for boys. That's unfortunate, because kids
learn a lot as they construct block cities, roads, and
fortresses. One study found that girls are less likely
to be found in advanced physics classes because they
don't play with blocks as much as boys do.

Unfortunately, the block corner can be the scene
of territorial struggles—with the "regulars" staking
out claims, excluding girls as well as boys who are
not part of the block clique. Watch carefully for the
dynamics in your play group to make sure that both
boys and girls have access to blocks. One research
study found that in classrooms, if a teacher posi-
tions himself or herself in the block corner, girls are
more likely to enter and engage in play.

ABC Play Group Chatter

Before I toss something in the trash, I
think how it could be used for play group.
I took a large plastic box and started sav-
ing old shirts for art smocks, discarded
jackets for dress-up, used greeting cards
for possible art projects, and so forth.

—Amy, mother of two

Playing with blocks builds a strong scientific and mathematical foundation. It also helps build a child's self-esteem, encourages his creativity and imagination, and fosters small motor skills.

When building with blocks, a child learns about gravity, stability, weight, balance, and systems. She learns about inductive thinking, discovery, the properties of matter, and the interaction of forces. In short, there's a lot of learning going on as those block cities are going up.

Math skills are also being developed in the block corner. A child learns about depth, width, height, length, measurement, volume, area, classification, shape, symmetry, mapping, equality (same as), and inequality (more than, less than).

Art concepts such as patterns, symmetry, and balance are also learned from building with blocks. Prereading skills such as shape recognition, differentiation of shapes, and size relations are educational byproducts of block building.

By the way, not only is building with blocks educational—but cleanup is, also! Sorting and storing blocks teaches classification and one-to-one correspondence.

Dramatic Play

Playing house and dress-up is fun and educational. This kind of dramatic play encourages a child's imagination and creativity. It also brings the grown-up world down to size and helps a child process what he sees around him.

One of the unexpected effects of dramatic play is that it encourages a child to be more flexible. He learns to substitute a pretend item for the real thing. For example, empty paper towel rolls transform into telescopes for little pirates, batons for budding maestros, or even an elephant's trunk if the kids are playing zoo animals.

Through imaginative play, children can also try out emotions and feelings. For example, one little boy, following the death of a beloved grandfather, organized his play group friends to reenact a funeral for a stuffed animal. This gave him an opportunity to work through some of the rituals and emotions that he saw and felt.

ABC Play Group Chatter

Research has shown that children who participate in pretend play are usually more joyful and cooperative, more willing to share and take turns, and have larger vocabularies than children who don't often participate in pretend play.

Manipulative Toys

Kids get better at printing not by copying letters on a blank sheet but by playing with manipulative toys. Play items like Legos, Bristle Blocks, Play-Doh, Peg Board, beads to thread, and stacking or nesting materials help develop a child's fine motor skills. That kind of muscle control is necessary for learning how to write.

Often, these toys are used in fantasy play. For example, the child creates a zoo filled with animals made from Play-Doh. Encourage youngsters to stretch their creativity by combining toys. For example, kids could build zoo buildings with blocks and then fill them with the clay animals they've created.

A child needs a strong and stable trunk (the part of the body from neck to legs) to learn to write. Fun activities such as walking like a crab (the child sits on the floor, hands on the floor behind him, and lifts up his bottom) or like a bear (hands and feet on the floor and walking) strengthen a youngster's trunk and back.

Puzzles

Puzzles are great brain food. Whether complex or simple, interlocking or individually slotted, puzzles help develop abstract thinking. Kids learn how to look at a space and envision what belongs there. Playing with puzzles helps refine a child's fine motor control, which is essential to push the puzzle pieces into place.

Play Group Do's

Have a range of puzzles available to the group. Some kids want the challenge of attempting more complex puzzles while others enjoy doing simple puzzles because they gain a sense of accomplishment from easily completing them.

Outdoor Play

If possible, play groups should try to include outdoor time. Whether it's in the backyard or in a nearby park, running, swinging, climbing, jumping, hopping, digging in the sand, and looking at nature, are all fun activities and provide a wealth of educational opportunities.

Outdoor play helps develop a child's gross motor skills (the large muscle groups). In fact, those muscles and cross-lateral movement (right arm/left leg and vice-versa) are also important for learning to read and write. Outdoor time provides opportunities to explore and manipulate different environments.

Kids' imaginations are also stretched as they participate in fantasy play while getting physical. The jungle gym becomes a castle; the swings are airplanes or rocket ships.

And of course, outdoor play is perfect for burning off excess energy!

Cooking

No matter how the dish turns out, kids enjoy cooking and learn a lot, too. It's the process rather than the result that is important. Cooking also helps build a child's self-esteem and sense of competency because it's a life skill that grown-ups perform on a daily basis.

Math skills are key components in cooking. Young cooks measure and count ingredients. Science learning is also part of the experience as children discover how things change if you alter the environment. Liquid batter becomes solid cake when baked; juice cups become popsicles when frozen. Kids also learn cause and effect relationships. If they don't put the juice cups in the freezer, then they won't become popsicles.

And then, there's deductive reasoning: how can I hold the frozen juice popsicle to eat it? Do I put a stick in the cup before freezing? Do I wait until the juice cup is partially frozen and then insert the stick? At which point does the stick stand up straighter?

Play Group Do's

Cooking with children is an excellent opportunity to discuss nutrition. Kids learn about which foods are good for you, which give you energy, raw ingredients versus processed foods, and more.

Fine motor skills are also being put to use when cooking. Stirring, chopping, and adding ingredients slowly, all exercise the small muscle groups.

Free Play

Play groups may choose to have a planned activity for each session, but there should also be time for the children to choose their own adventures. Free play doesn't mean time off for the parents in charge of that day's gathering. Left to their own devices, kids may each find a toy and settle in to play alone or compatibly with a friend—or battles may erupt over toys, frustration can mount over puzzle pieces that don't fit, and dramatic play can become … well, dramatic! So the adults in charge need to keep a close eye and be ready with a helping hand or small suggestion to facilitate the free play portion of the day.

Free play—whatever activity a child chooses—is an opportunity for a youngster to learn about decision-making and the consequences of those choices. "If I make a painting, then I won't have time to build with the blocks." Children also learn about time management: "If I do this puzzle, will I have time to play dress-up?"

Cooperative Play

Depending on the ages of the children in the group, you may see a lot of parallel play and little cooperative play. The ability to work together and take turns develops as the kids mature. But under adult direction, you may be able to encourage full-group activities. For example, each child could paint his own picture, but together they could create an art show and explain their drawings to the group.

ABC Play Group Chatter

Clyde Robinson, Ph.D., professor of child development at Brigham Young University, advises that young children often use parallel play to ease into a group. For example, a preschooler will play next to a group engaged together in play in the block corner, then make an attempt to join the group.

Cooperative play teaches children to respect each other and helps develop social skills. Kids learn to share, albeit not always graciously. They also learn how to work together to accomplish a shared goal—such as building the tallest block tower ever!

Sand/Water Table or at a Playground

There are institutional-quality sand tables that can also double as water basins. Essentially sandboxes with legs, these are lots of fun, and many preschools and daycare facilities invest in them because sand/water play is soothing and educational. But homemade versions—a big basin or an outdoor sandbox—can accomplish the same thing.

The nice thing about playing with water and sand is that there is not a "right" way to do it (except it's definitely wrong to throw it on the floor or at each other). Each child experiences success and uses her imagination to manipulate the sand/water for her own fantasy play.

Pouring, packing, and digging help develop fine motor skills and eye-hand coordination. Kids also learn math concepts. For example, while having fun pouring water from one container to another, they also discover how many cups of water it takes to fill a quart-size pitcher (or conversely, how many cups can be filled from the water in a quart-size pitcher). Science is also part of the experience as they discover the causes and effects of certain actions. For example, what happens to a dry sponge when it's dipped into water?

Books: Reading Together and Alone

Besides the obvious inherent educational value found in the information contained in books, the processes of an adult reading to a group of children—as well as a child reading to himself—are also learning experiences.

Group experiences are lessons in social skills. The child learns to sit quietly, listen intently, and absorb and process information. As a child "reads" to himself, he is actually acquiring prereading skills as he learns to track words across the page—even if he can't decode them yet.

Cleanup

At the end of every play group session, all children should help clean up. Even if it's probably more efficient for the grownups to zip through the cleanup afterward, you want the children to participate. Adults may have to direct the process, but kids learn that neatness and helping are valued behaviors. As they sort the toys, putting the blocks in a container, stuffed animals in a basket, and books on the shelves they also learn about classification and organization.

Cleanup teaches self-discipline and even cause and effect. If you know where you put the toy, you can find it the next time. If you take good care of the book, you'll have it to read another day. It's another group behavior where the kids can chat with each other, discussing the best way to clean up (which of course strengthens their verbal skills).

The Least You Need to Know

- Through play, children acquire the fundamental skills they need to learn to read and perform mathematical calculations.
- Sophisticated scientific concepts are learned as children play with blocks and cook.
- Play helps develop a child's social and communication skills.
- Cleanup at the end of the play group session is also a valuable educational experience.

Resources

Websites

www.aap.org This is the website for the American Academy of Pediatrics, with a comprehensive section for parents.

www.americanbaby.com This site has play group information and articles of interest to parents.

www.babycenter.com This comprehensive site has topics of interest to parents of babies, toddlers, and preschoolers. It's also an excellent resource for pregnancy information.

www.cdc.gov This is the website of the Centers for Disease Control and Prevention, which includes health information for all stages of life.

www.child-abuse.com This site provides links to child abuse hotlines in every state.

www.clubmom.com This comprehensive site has articles of interest and message boards for parents.

www.cpsc.gov The U.S. Consumer Product Safety Commission website provides a wide range of information on product safety standards and much more. You can subscribe to free e-mail announcements of safety news and product recalls.

www.naeyc.org The National Association for the Education of Young Children promotes excellence in early childhood education. Its website offers resources for families, including information on quality childcare programs, preschool, or schools for children as well as activities parents and caregivers can do at home to encourage a child's development.

www.parenting.com This comprehensive site has lots of resources for parents.

www.parenting.ivillage.com Part of iVillage, this site offers information about babies, toddlers, and preschoolers (the website also has information about older children). Parents can join individualized message boards to interact with other families who have children the same age.

www.womenshealth.gov/violence/state This comprehensive site offers state-by-state domestic violence resources.

Books

Baylies, Peter. *Stay-at-Home Dad Handbook*. Chicago: Chicago Review Press, 2004.

Egan, Mary, Amy Freedman, Judi Greenberg, and Sharon Anderson. *Is It a Big Problem or a Little Problem?* New York: St. Martin's Griffin, 2007.

Ellison, Sheila. *365 Games Smart Toddlers Play.* Naperville, IL: Sourcebooks, 2006.

Schulman, Nancy and Ellen Birnbaum. *Practical Wisdom for Parents: Demystifying the Preschool Years.* New York: Alfred A. Knopf, 2007.

Worrell, Nancy. *The Complete Idiot's Guide to Backyard Adventures.* Indianapolis: Alpha Books, 2008.

Index

B

P